BUILDING A STRONG FOUNDATION

D1450367

BUILDING A STRONG FOUNDATION

FUNDRAISING FOR NONPROFITS

Richard L. Edwards
Elizabeth A. S. Benefield
with
Jeffrey A. Edwards
John A. Yankey

NASW PRESS

National Association of Social Workers
Washington, DC

Jay J. Cayner, ACSW, LSW, *President*
Josephine Nieves, MSW, PhD, *Executive Director*

Linda Beebe, *Executive Editor*
Nancy Winchester, *Editorial Services Director*
Patricia D. Wolf, Wolf Publications, Inc., *Copy Editor*
Ronald W. Wolf, Wolf Publications, Inc., *Copy Editor*
Marcia A. Metzgar, Wolf Publications, Inc., *Proofreader*
Beth Gyorgy, Shenandoah Publications, Inc., *Proofreader*
Bernice Eisen, *Indexer*

Library of Congress Cataloging-in-Publication Data
Edwards, Richard L.
    Building a strong foundation : fundraising for nonprofits / Richard L. Edwards, Elizabeth A.S. Benefield with Jeffrey A. Edwards, John A. Yankey.
      p.   cm.
    Includes bibliographical references and index.
    ISBN 0-87101-249-9 (alk. paper)
    1. Nonprofit organizations—United States—Finance. 2. Fund raising. I. Benefield, Elizabeth A. S. II. Title.
HG4027.65.E34   1996
658.15′224—dc21   96-37011
                                          CIP

Printed in the United States of America

DEDICATION

We dedicate this book to Emily Grace Benefield, who was born on November 15, 1995, as this book was being written. We hope that she and others of her generation grow to adulthood in a world marked by civility, peace, and social justice.

R.L.E., E.A.S.B., J.A.E., and J.A.Y.

CONTENTS

PREFACE

Professional fundraisers and nonprofit leaders seeking help on how to raise funds effectively for their organizations will find no shortage of advice. A multitude of books, journals, newsletters, and other publications, as well as workshops, exist to instruct on everything from launching special campaigns to the art of writing winning proposals. Entire books are available on such topics as major gift cultivation and special event fundraising.

All of this "intelligence" is useful for the fundraising profession and for nonprofits. Fundraising for nonprofits is a fast-growing field and, generally, individuals who demonstrate success in fundraising are highly marketable.

However, the authors of this book recognize that many individuals in the nonprofit community do not know where to begin seeking help, are overwhelmed by the plethora and cost of resource materials, and are often intimidated by the tasks associated with raising money. We also recognize that many individuals raising funds for nonprofits are serving their organization in other roles, often as executive directors or board members. We therefore sought to make this book concise, readable, and relevant.

Our many years of experience in fundraising have taught us that two important principles should guide our efforts. First, we believe that fundraising is a *process* that has at its core donor relationships that are nurtured over a long time. Second, multifaceted fundraising strategies are required to ensure your nonprofit long-term prosperity and fiscal stability.

The fundraising process is dynamic and people-driven. You will not find in this book a formula or step-by-step manual. Rather, we offer you something analogous to an old family recipe. Family members over the years may alter slightly or personalize the recipe to reflect individual tastes, but the basic ingredients remain unchanged. In fundraising, you must be creative in personalizing your approaches to donors, but at the same time, you must keep in mind some time-tested truths. Many of these "truths" or strategies are discussed in this book. Most are connected in some way to the successful cultivation of a donor relationship. Others relate to the importance of maintaining diverse fundraising activities that (1) include both annual fund and major gift work; (2) encourage the cultivation of individual, foundation, and corporate donors; and (3) support the premise that building a strong foundation takes time, resources, and good planning.

We include a comprehensive chapter in this book about prospect research, an important area in fundraising that is often overlooked in the literature. It is our belief that good research is an essential component of all successful fundraising programs. With the availability of new information technologies, prospect research is an area of rapid change and growth.

We also include a chapter on planned giving. Nonprofits have much to gain by exploring ways to secure planned gifts. We believe that even the novice fundraiser or nonprofit executive will find the information and tips in this chapter to be understandable and useful.

Finally, we explore cause-related marketing as a method to raise funds. Still in its infancy, cause-related marketing, as part of a multifaceted fundraising program, promises to be a viable and profitable way for many nonprofits to succeed in raising dollars.

We sincerely hope that this book will be a useful resource for those of you already raising money for important causes, and for those of you just getting started. We know that fundraising is tough work. We also know that success in fundraising has enormous rewards. Nothing can compare with the exhilarating joy and magic that happen when you help someone realize a dream, memorialize or honor a loved one, or make a heartfelt contribution. We wish you many of those times.

R.L.E., E.A.S.B., J.A.E., and J.A.Y.

ACKNOWLEDGMENTS

There are many people who deserve our thanks for assisting us, both directly and indirectly, in the preparation of this book. We first wish to thank Mary Altpeter and Sylvia Yankey for taking the time to read various drafts of the manuscript and providing us with helpful suggestions based on their years of fundraising experience. We also wish to thank Randy Benefield for his support throughout the project.

We were fortunate to receive a great deal of technical support throughout the development of this book. In particular, we wish to thank several people at the University of North Carolina at Chapel Hill (UNC-CH) School of Social Work, including John McMahon for his assistance in preparing many of the figures included in the book, Daniel Lebold for his ongoing support, Robert Hawkins for his editing suggestions, and Maxcine Barnes and Anne-Marie Sullivan for their secretarial assistance throughout the writing of this book. From the UNC-CH Office of Development, we thank June Steel, Director of Planned Giving, for contributing the chapter entitled "Fundamentals of Planned Giving."

The technical support we received during the writing and production processes was invaluable. We thank our publisher, Linda Beebe, and director of editorial resources, Nancy Winchester, both at NASW Press, for their flexibility, encouragement, and occasional prodding. Without their efforts, this book would not have come into being. We also thank Patricia and Ronald Wolf, at Wolf Publications, for their expert editing services.

Finally, we want to acknowledge the contributions of many people who have helped us to become effective fundraisers. These include a variety of mentors, nonprofit executives and board members, donors, and students in our classes and workshops. Over the years, these individuals have taught us a great deal about the art and science of fundraising, including the importance of building relationships and other tools and techniques that lead to success. We thank all of those who have taught us, motivated us, and inspired us. We are particularly grateful to John A. Tate, Jr., founding chairperson of the UNC-CH School of Social Work's board of advisors, and John B. Turner, dean emeritus both of the UNC-CH School of Social Work and Case Western Reserve University's Mandel School of Applied Social Sciences. They represent the very best example of how volunteers and professionals can collaborate for successful fundraising. They have been excellent role models and their wise counsel has been of immense value over the years. Furthermore, we want to express our appreciation to Matthew Kupec, UNC-CH's vice chancellor for development and university advancement, for his valued support.

To all of those who have helped us specifically with this book, as well as those who over time taught us so many valuable lessons about fundraising, we give full credit for our strengths as fundraisers; for our shortcomings, we take full responsibility.

R.L.E., E.A.S.B., J.A.E., and J.A.Y.

CHAPTER 1

THE CONTEXT OF FUNDRAISING

Nonprofit organizations have played, and will continue to play, vital roles in nearly every aspect of our lives. In the areas of health and human services, advocacy, and the arts, nonprofits are numerous, and their contributions to the well-being of our nation can hardly be overstated. Although government organizations are increasingly contracting with nonprofits to deliver various services they are mandated to provide, donations from individuals, corporations, and foundations are still critical to the fiscal health of nonprofits.

In 1995 total giving to tax-exempt nonprofits in the United States was estimated to exceed $143.8 billion (Kaplan, 1996). Estimates for 1996 suggest that giving to nonprofits from all sources may reach a new high of $150 billion (Panas, 1996). During recent decades, contributions from individuals, both living and through bequests, and by foundations and corporations made up 2 percent of our nation's gross domestic product (Kaplan, 1995). Private or voluntary contributions from individuals, foundations, and corporations provide approximately 20 percent of the total revenue for all nonprofits combined (Kaplan, 1993). However, many nonprofits, particularly grassroots and smaller organizations, rely more heavily on voluntary contributions. Even larger nonprofits find they must increasingly rely on voluntary or private giving.

Nonprofit organizations exist in a rapidly changing environment, one that constantly threatens their financial stability. Individuals will contribute varying amounts to your nonprofit organization, depending on many factors, including how they view their own financial situation. Changes in federal and state budget priorities, with concomitant reductions in spending levels for many areas where nonprofits are involved, such as the arts, education, environment, health, and human services, have created a more competitive environment for philanthropic dollars. To ensure that your nonprofit survives and thrives in the years ahead, you will need to implement multifaceted fundraising strategies that will broaden your base of supporters. By concentrating on building a solid base of donor support, you can enable your nonprofit to gain an important competitive edge.

We believe that fundraising for nonprofits must be approached in a strategic manner that involves a variety of components. In our experience, fundraising is the process that builds a solid foundation for your nonprofit. Fundraising is an investment in your organization's future that will result in a greater degree of permanence and stability.

A primary goal of any good, comprehensive fundraising strategy is to identify and cultivate a network of individual, foundation, and corporate funders. Although you should seek to develop a base of donors who will make annual gifts, you should have major gift fundraising strategies in place as well. Your aim each year should be to maintain most of your regular supporters while at the same time bringing in new donors. As Meyers (1989) suggests, your nonprofit's success in fundraising may be measured by several different yardsticks:

- whether you have reached or exceeded your specific fundraising goals
- whether your nonprofit's visibility has increased
- whether your primary constituencies and potential donor populations have positive reactions to your organization as a result of your fundraising efforts.

Success in fundraising requires time, persistence, and a strong ego to withstand rejections. Many valid requests for funding and many excellent proposals get turned down for a variety of reasons that have little to do with the worth of your cause or the quality of your appeal.

In this chapter, we consider current patterns of giving to nonprofits by individuals, corporations, and foundations, as well as factors that motivate giving. We also address the changing donor demographics and ethical considerations in fundraising.

CURRENT PATTERNS OF GIVING

For you to develop a successful fundraising program, you must first understand the sources of philanthropic dollars. Many people believe that nonprofits get most of their money from corporations and foundations. In reality, foundation and corporate giving makes up only 12.4 percent of giving to nonprofits, with the remaining 87.6 percent provided by individuals (Kaplan, 1996). The total giving for individuals includes gifts that come to nonprofits after a donor's death in the form of bequests (6.8 percent) and gifts from living individuals (80.8 percent). In 1995 the total giving by individuals, including bequests, was $126 billion (Kaplan, 1996). Giving to nonprofits by individuals in the United States is more than seven times that of corporations and foundations. Yet, many nonprofits overlook individuals when they develop their fundraising plans.

Because individuals provide such a high percentage of contributions to nonprofits, you should devote significant attention to developing effective strategies to attract individual donors. At the same time, you should not ignore foundations and corporations. Although foundations and corporations provide only a small percentage of the overall support to nonprofits, they are nonetheless extremely important sources of revenue.

Generally, foundations and corporations provide funding for specific programs and activities and less often give unrestricted funds or funds for endowments. Although this method of funding can be limiting, foundation and corporate dollars can be important in augmenting other forms of support for your nonprofit and can, in various ways, help to promote your organizational mission.

Although a small part of the total, donations by foundations have increased dramatically in recent years. During the first half of the current decade, giving by foundations increased at a greater rate than giving by individuals and corporations combined (Kaplan, 1995). This increase in giving is the result of several factors. In recent years, the asset bases of many foundations have increased, providing them with more dollars to allocate. Additionally, more foundations have been created. This trend began during the 1980s when more than 3,000 foundations were created, each with assets of more than $1 million or annual grant budgets that exceeded $100,000. Overall, the assets of foundations increased threefold during the 1980s because of the combined effect of the rise in the value of assets of existing foundations and the creation of new foundations.

In 1995 U.S. foundations made contributions totaling $10.44 billion, whereas giving by corporations and corporate foundations totaled approximately $7.4 billion. However, cutbacks in government funding for nonprofit organizations and the dramatic growth in the number of nonprofits being created to meet societal needs have meant heightened competition for corporate and foundation grants.

A recent survey by *The Chronicle of Philanthropy* (Gray & Moore, 1996a) suggests that corporate giving to nonprofits is increasing. Although corporate giving rose by an average of only 2.9 percent from 1994 to 1995 (not much more than the rate of inflation during that period), the average increase for 1995 was 7.5 percent, which was far ahead of the rate of inflation. This increase in giving is attributed to significant growth in profits. Although profits are increasing, at the same time many corporations are reducing the size of their philanthropy staffs or contracting with outside companies to administer their philanthropic programs (Gray & Moore, 1996b). Figure 1-1 shows the sources of contributions to nonprofits.

More than 1 million organizations make up the nonprofit sector in the United States (Kaplan, 1995). The major categories of nonprofits receiving voluntary contributions from individuals, foundations, and corporations include religion, education, human services, health, and the arts. Figure 1-2 shows where voluntary contributions went in 1995.

Nonprofit organizations differ in the extent to which they rely on gifts and grants for their revenue. Smaller nonprofits rely most heavily on such contributions. Those organizations with assets of less than $100,000 receive approximately 58 percent of their revenue from such sources, whereas those with assets of more than $50 million rely on such sources for only

FIGURE 1-1. SOURCES OF CONTRIBUTIONS TO NONPROFITS IN 1995

Total Giving: $143.85 billion

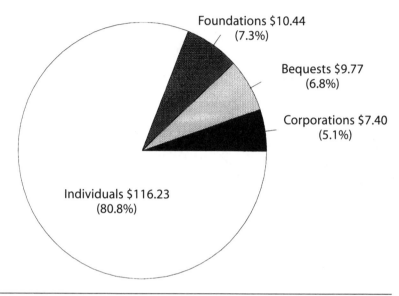

Foundations $10.44 (7.3%)

Bequests $9.77 (6.8%)

Corporations $7.40 (5.1%)

Individuals $116.23 (80.8%)

NOTE: *Figures are given in billions of dollars. Source: Kaplan, A. E. (Ed.). (1996). Giving USA—1996. New York: AAFRC Trust for Philanthropy. Reprinted with permission.*

about 11 percent of their revenue. The larger nonprofits rely heavily on program service revenue. However, even for the largest nonprofits, charitable contributions are critical for certain functions. Thus, whether your nonprofit is large or small, whether it is new or has been in existence for many years, you are likely to need to be involved with fundraising.

UNDERSTANDING WHY PEOPLE GIVE

At its most basic, fundraising involves asking people to give to a particular cause. This is true whether you are dealing with individuals, foundations, or corporations, because the latter two represent collections of individuals. Your primary challenge as a fundraiser "lies in finding sufficient numbers of persons who can be motivated and influenced

FIGURE 1-2. USES OF CONTRIBUTIONS TO NONPROFITS IN 1995

Total Giving: $143.85 billion

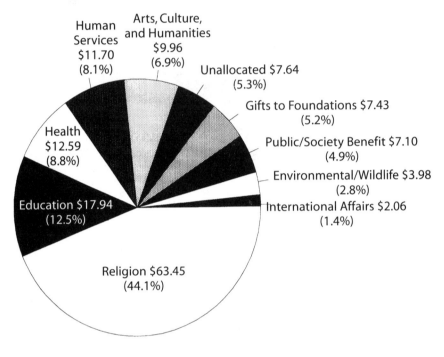

NOTE: *Figures are given in billions of dollars. Source: Kaplan, A. E. (Ed.). (1996). Giving USA—1996. New York: AAFRC Trust for Philanthropy. Reprinted with permission.*

to give, who are capable of giving the requisite dollars, and who can be interested in the purposes and needs to be served" (Mixer, 1993, p. 3). As shown in Figure 1-3, you need to consider potential donors in terms of capacity, motivation, and opportunity. First, identify those who have sufficient giving capacity. Second, motivate those individuals or philanthropic organizations to give to your particular cause. Finally, give prospective donors the opportunity to contribute. In short, ask prospective donors in a tactful manner to give at an appropriate level. In succeeding chapters, we discuss how to identify prospects with the capacity to make significant gifts and how to implement appropriate

FIGURE 1-3. THE DONOR GIVING TRIANGLE

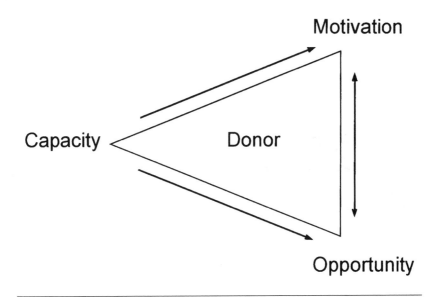

strategies to secure those gifts. For now, let us turn our attention to the matter of motivation.

Although 28 percent of the U.S. adult population do not give to any charitable or philanthropic causes (Mixer, 1993), 72 percent of all adults do give (Hodgkinson, Weitzman, Noga, & Gorski, 1992). Some of those people may give to a wide range of nonprofit organizations or causes, whereas others give to only one or two.

The reasons people give to nonprofits are multiple and complex, ranging from religious beliefs and guilt to pride and peer pressure (Mixer, 1993). Many experienced fundraisers suggest that donors typically have multiple and varied motivations for giving (Broce, 1986; Huntsinger, 1982; Panas, 1984; Schneiter, 1985). This theory is confirmed by research conducted by the Gallup Organization for the Independent Sector (Hodgkinson et al., 1992) in which respondents listed the 11 motives for giving funds and volunteering their time to nonprofit causes (see Table 1-1).

TABLE 1-1. REASONS PEOPLE GIVE TO NONPROFIT ORGANIZATIONS

Reason	Percentage
Those with more should help those with less	55
Gained personal satisfaction from giving and volunteering	43
Met religious beliefs or commitments	41
Benefits derived from giving back to society	39
Was asked to contribute or volunteer by personal friend or business associate	36
Ensured continuation of activities or institutions from which they or their family benefit	34
Served as an example to others	31
Fulfilled a business or community obligation	19
Created a remembrance of oneself or one's family	17
Obtained tax considerations and deductions	12
Was encouraged by an employer	10

NOTE: *Scores total more than 100 percent because some respondents gave multiple answers.* Source: *Hodgkinson, V. A., Weitzman, M. S., Noga, S. M., & Gorski, H. A. (1992). Giving and volunteering in the United States: Findings from a national survey. Washington, DC: Independent Sector.*

The various motives given represent three themes. The first four motives relate to a sense of one's personal responsibility to others, whereas the second four are oriented to one's relationships with others. The final three motives relate to personal benefits, such as receiving recognition or tax breaks or pleasing an employer.

Interestingly, and perhaps not surprisingly, volunteering is an important element in giving behavior. Those who volunteer are more likely to give, and more likely to give at higher levels, than those who do not volunteer. In fact, 90 percent of the individuals who volunteer for a nonprofit organization also contribute money to nonprofits, whereas only 59 percent of those who do not volunteer make financial contributions (Kaplan, 1995). The Independent Sector (Hodgkinson et al., 1992) found that households with members who both volunteered and gave money made gifts that averaged two and one-half times the average contributions from households that did not volunteer. This finding suggests that you should find ways to involve prospective donors in your nonprofit so they become invested in it. Such involvement might include recruiting them to serve on boards or committees, help with a special event, or volunteer in some other capacity.

Other factors also influence giving. Socioeconomic status clearly has an impact on giving behavior. Families who have financial worries or concerns give approximately one-third less than those who do not have such concerns. Those who itemize their tax returns, and thus claim tax deductions for charitable contributions, outgive those who do not itemize taxes by about four to one. People who either give a percentage of their incomes or pledge specific amounts give larger sums than those with less systematic giving patterns (Hodgkinson et al., 1992).

In a seminal study of reasons why people make large gifts to nonprofits, Panas (1984) compared the views and attitudes of individuals who made gifts of $1 million with the views of nonprofit professionals. The nonprofit professionals included fundraisers and executives and represented health, education, religious, and cultural organizations, as well as the YMCA and the Salvation Army. For the $1 million donors, the top giving motivators are listed in Table 1-2.

TABLE 1-2. TOP GIVING MOTIVATORS FOR $1 MILLION DONORS

Motivators	Rating
Belief in the mission of the institution	9.6
Community responsibility and civic pride	8.1
Fiscal stability of the institution	7.4
Regard for staff leadership	7.4
Respect for the institution locally	7.0
Regard for volunteer leadership of institution	6.7
Serves on the board of trustees, a major committee, or other official body of the institution	6.5
Respect for the institution in a wider circle—region, nation, state	6.2

NOTE: *Rating stated is the average rating on 10-point scale, with 10 being the highest and 1 being the lowest.*

TABLE 1-3. AVERAGE RATINGS OF THE TOP MOTIVATORS AS VIEWED BY THE FUNDRAISING PROFESSIONALS

Motivator	Rating
Belief in the mission of the institution	7.9
Great interest in a specific program within the project	7.6
Involvement in the campaign program	6.9
Serves on the board of trustees, a major committee, or other official body of the institution	6.9
Memorial opportunity	6.9
Respect for the institution locally	6.9
Has an adult history of being involved in the institution	6.8
Leverage or influence of the solicitor	6.8

NOTE: *Rating stated is the average rating on 10-point scale, with 10 being the highest and 1 being the lowest.*

Listed in Table 1-3 are the average ratings of the top motivators as viewed by the fundraising professionals.

Both the $1 million givers and the fundraising professionals viewed "belief in the mission of the institution" as the top motivator for giving. In addition, both groups thought it important to be involved with the recipient institution or organization, and both were concerned with the respect the organization commanded. Panas (1984), however, points out some important differences between the two categories of participants. The $1 million givers, for instance, were highly motivated by a sense of community responsibility and civic pride. They also were concerned about the fiscal stability of the organization and the quality of the organization's staff and volunteer leadership. The professionals, however, believed donors were motivated by their interest in specific programs or activities, were more likely to give if they were involved in the campaign program, or had an adult history of involvement with the institution. Furthermore, the professionals believed that the givers were motivated by memorial opportunities and the influence of the solicitor.

What factors the $1 million givers and the professionals saw as less significant also is important, and here we see much common ground. The reasons rated as least important by the $1 million givers are shown in Table 1-4. The reasons rated as least important by professional fundraisers are shown in Table 1-5.

TABLE 1-4. REASONS FOR GIVING RATED AS LEAST IMPORTANT BY $1 MILLION DONORS

Reason	Rating
Guilt feelings	1.3
Appeal and drama of the campaign material requesting the gift	2.3
Tax considerations	2.4

NOTE: *Rating stated is the average rating on 10-point scale, with 10 being the highest and 1 being the lowest.*

Clearly, guilt feelings and slick campaign materials are not likely to motivate either large or small gifts. In addition, tax considerations are not important motivators for $1 million donors. However, tax considerations are not irrelevant for all major gift prospects. Large gifts are rarely made without some consideration of tax advantages, even though this is not the primary motivation for the gift.

Panas (1984) found that $1 million donors identified another important influence on their giving behavior: "Each donor spoke about the joy they experience in their giving. The magical and glowing ecstasy" (pp. 210–211). Panas suggests that nonprofit organizations too often neglect the "exhilaration and the joy" related to giving. He goes on to say, "no single factor plays the dominant, overriding motivation. It is indeed most often a serendipitous confluence of a number of factors" (p. 211).

TABLE 1-5. REASONS FOR GIVING RATED AS LEAST IMPORTANT BY FUNDRAISING PROFESSIONALS

Reason	Rating
Guilt feelings	2.7
Appeal and drama of the campaign material requesting the gift	4.1
Fiscal stability of the institution	4.2

NOTE: *Rating stated is the average rating on 10-point scale, with 10 being the highest and 1 being the lowest.*

A review of the giving motivations of donors shows that they clearly make contributions both because of internal motivations and external influences. The internal motivations have three dimensions—personal, social, and negative, or what some term the "I", "we," and "they" factors. The personal or "I" factors include such things as self-esteem, achievement, cognitive interest, personal growth, guilt reduction or avoidance, search for meaning or purpose in life, personal gain or benefit, spirituality, sense of immortality, or survival. The social or "we" factors include status, affiliation, group endeavor, interdependence, altruism, family and offspring, and power. The negative or "they" factors include frustration, unknown situations, insecurity, fear and anxiety, and complexity. We find that people are more likely to become donors when they are treated well during the fundraising process, when they are interested in the organization or cause, and when they get rewarded for their support in ways that are consistent with their own values and motivations. Tapping into negative motivations, such as through the use of scare tactics, is an almost certain recipe for failure in fundraising.

External influences also include three dimensions—rewards, stimulations, and situations. Rewards can be recognition and other personal or social benefits. Stimulations are human needs, personal requests, vision, private initiative, efficiency and effectiveness, and tax deductions. Situations may include personal involvement, planning and decision making, peer pressure, networks, family involvement, culture, tradition, role identity, and disposable income. To be successful, you must understand the myriad factors that motivate donors to give and structure your fundraising approaches accordingly.

UNDERSTANDING WHY PEOPLE DO NOT GIVE

As you devise strategies that will enhance or increase donor motivation, you also may find it useful to consider some of the reasons why people do not give. The rationales indicated by household respondents who had stopped giving to a particular charity are given in Table 1-6.

When asked their views on why people do not give, several thousand participants in more than 100 fundraising workshops offered a variety of

TABLE 1-6. REASONS PEOPLE GAVE FOR NOT CONTRIBUTING TO CHARITY

Reason	Percentage
Lack of money	25
Lack of trust in the charity	24
Charity's misuse of funds	17
Disagreement with the charity or lack of similar beliefs	7
The charity's fundraising techniques or "pestering me"	6
Gave to another organization	5
Don't know	4
Other miscellaneous reasons	17

NOTE: *Scores total more than 100 percent because of multiple responses by some respondents. Source: Independent Sector survey (Hodgkinson, V. A., Weitzman, M. S., Noga, S. M., & Gorski, H. A. [1992]).* Giving and volunteering in the United States: Findings from a national survey. *Washington, DC: Independent Sector.*

reasons that cluster around four problems of donor–organization relations: (1) personal characteristics and situations; (2) communications; (3) reactions to solicitations; and (4) organizational image (Hodgkinson et al., 1992).

The personal characteristics and situations that can be a detriment to giving include personal preferences, contrary beliefs, dislike of programs, financial considerations, and situational reasons. Personal preferences are such things as higher priorities, lack of concern for or lack of interest in the organization, and lack of involvement. Contrary beliefs include disagreement with the organization's mission, disagreement on policies, and lack of belief in the cause. Dislike of programs includes differences in values and work ethic. Financial considerations include people being unable to afford to give and general economic conditions and tax rates. Situations that adversely affect giving include personal life complexities, competition for limited donor dollars, changing environments, and donors' reluctance to give outside of their geographic area.

The respondents identified two types of communication problems as detrimental to giving: lack of information and ineffective communication. Lack of information is characterized by unfamiliarity with the organization and its mission, lack of support by staff and others, and an unclear record of service or demonstration of financial needs. Ineffective communication includes negative publicity and the perception by the prospective donor that the organization's needs are not clear, its publications are too slick, and its promotions too costly.

Unsuccessful requests or asks can be attributed to such problems as the manner of asking, the solicitor, relations with the prospect, and timing. The manner of asking is a problem when the prospective donor is asked too often or asked the wrong way, when the donor senses that he or she is being manipulated, or when there are too many mailings. Donors tend not to give if they do not like the asker, if they have no sense of obligation to the asker, when organizations use paid solicitors, or when the wrong person makes the ask. Relations with the prospect can be a problem when there is no personal contact, no recognition for past gifts or sense of appreciation, when the prospective donor is not asked to give, or when there is no tradition of giving. Timing is a problem when the donor already gave, is asked too late, or is asked at the wrong time.

Finally, organizational image problems include perceptions of poor organizational behavior and issues that relate to management. Perceptions of poor organizational behavior include active mistrust, a perception that the agency is "too rich" or has high administrative costs, a bad experience with the organization, a poor public reputation, a sense that services cost too much, the perception of duplication of services, government involvement, or the perception that taxes pay for services. Management issues include perceptions that gifts are misused, the organization has poor policies and rules, the fundraising costs are high, and the organization has poor leadership. All of the foregoing concerns suggest that you must be concerned about the credibility of your nonprofit and its management staff.

CHANGING DONOR DEMOGRAPHICS

As a fundraiser, you must be cognizant of the fact that the population is undergoing dramatic demographic and ethnic change. By 2000, 25 percent of the population of the United States is projected to be of Hispanic and African American ancestry. Furthermore, the proportion of the population that is of Asian ancestry will continue to increase, and it will constitute the fastest-growing segment of the population in many communities (Panas, 1996).

Many fundraisers believe that members of racial and ethnic groups tend not to be givers. However, evidence is increasing that members of racial and ethnic groups do give to organizations and causes "in which they are involved, where they have an active role, where their voice is truly heard" (Panas, 1996, pp. 15–16). The implications of this are obvious. If your nonprofit is going to be successful in fundraising, you must recognize and respond to changing demographic conditions. As Panas (1996) suggests, this means you must identify and reach out to those who have not traditionally been involved with your nonprofit and find ways to get them involved. In short, you must demonstrate to members of racial and ethnic groups that your nonprofit's mission addresses their concerns and needs and serves their community.

A great deal of wealth in this country will change hands over the next several years. It has been estimated that $11.4 trillion will be passed from one generation to another in the next seven years. Of special note, much of that wealth will be controlled by women (Panas, 1996). Not only are women beginning to control more money, they also are making the decisions about how it will be spent. According to a recent study of women and philanthropy (Sublett & Stone, 1993), an increasing number of women are electing to run family foundations or taking over the helm of family businesses. The report suggests that "a striking picture emerges of women in positions of financial power able for perhaps the first time in this century to become a dominant force in philanthropic activity" (p. 1). During the past 10 years or so, more women than men have earned bachelor's degrees; in fall 1990, more than 1 million more women than men were enrolled in U.S. colleges and universities. Perhaps as a result of greater educational opportunities leading to better jobs, women are giving more than ever before, a trend that can be expected to continue as they assume higher positions of leadership in the corporate and nonprofit sectors.

The "graying" of America also will have an impact on your fundraising efforts. The fastest-growing segment of the U.S. population is individuals who are 85 years of age and older. Soon, more than 100,000 men and women will be older than age 100 (Panas, 1996). An issue that may have an impact on their giving is that many of these older Americans are insecure about their finances because of concerns about health care needs and costs.

Baby boomers are now entering their 50s and will benefit from the huge wealth transfer that will take place in the next few years. Baby boomers must be approached somewhat differently from their elders. They tend to have less loyalty to a particular cause or organization than did their elders, seek opportunities that provide instant gratification, and want more information and accountability (Nichols, 1990). Although we must interpret these generalities with caution, clearly your nonprofit must be creative in developing strategies to involve this population group.

THE ETHICS OF FUNDRAISING

In recent years, more attention has been paid to ethical issues related to fundraising for nonprofit organizations. Periodic negative publicity regarding fundraising tactics, the costs of fundraising efforts, and the uses of funds raised has led to considerable discussion among those involved in legitimate fundraising activities. Such issues as confidentiality, conflict of interest, proper stewardship of funds, and compensation approaches for fundraisers have been debated extensively by nonprofit fundraisers. Out of these concerns and discussions have come statements of ethical principles that relate to individual fundraisers and donors, as well as to nonprofit organizations that are involved in fundraising.

The National Society of Fund Raising Executives (NSFRE) has adopted a *Code of Ethical Principles and Standards of Professional Practice* (Figure 1-4). A careful review of the ethical principles and standards included in the NSFRE code is a useful exercise for anyone considering becoming a fundraiser, whether as a professional, nonprofit executive, or nonprofit board member or volunteer. Such a review also can prove beneficial to organizations that are considering hiring a fundraising consultant or firm to assist them with their fundraising activities. We have found these principles and standards to be a helpful checklist as we have interviewed applicants for fundraising jobs or advised nonprofits on their consideration of fundraising consultants.

Just as attention to ethical issues related to fundraising professionals and fundraising activities has grown, interest has grown in the rights of donors. This interest led to the development of *A Donor Bill of Rights* (Figure 1-5).

We recommend that careful attention be paid to the rights of donors. Because fundraising is an activity that involves people, we must be concerned about how these people are treated. When donors are treated with respect, when their rights are considered and observed, they will generally feel that they have been well treated. Thus, assiduously observing their rights is not only the proper thing to do, it also will help lead to the ongoing success of an organization's fundraising efforts. Additionally, as seen in Table 1-2, the $1 million donors rated a number of factors related to the institution or organization as strong or important motivators, including belief in the mission of the organization; fiscal stability of the organization; regard for staff leadership; and respect for the institution locally, regionally, and nationally. Finally, when you treat your donors well, they will often want to continue to support your organization or cause. Conversely, when donors are not treated well, they are likely to discontinue their support, and word may get around and have a negative impact on giving by others.

In an effort to aid donors in making informed decisions about organizations, the National Charities Information Bureau (NCIB) has, for more than 75 years, been evaluating charitable organizations. Currently, the *NCIB Standards in Philanthropy* (NCIB, 1994), which were developed in the late 1980s, are used to rate national charitable organizations in terms of the following components:

* board governance
* purpose
* programs
* information

- financial support
- use of funds
- annual reporting
- accountability
- budget.

NCIB states that it believes the spirit of its standards makes them applicable to all charities, but it suggests that greater flexibility in applying some of the standards is appropriate for small organizations or those that are less than three years old. We concur with that assessment. The NCIB standards can be a useful template for judging how well your organization is structured for its fundraising efforts. In addition, NCIB publishes an informative quarterly newsletter, the *Wise Giving Guide*. To obtain a sample of the newsletter, a copy of the standards, or both, write to NCIB at 19 Union Square West, New York, NY 10003.

FIGURE 1-4. NSFRE CODE OF ETHICAL PRINCIPLES AND STANDARDS OF PROFESSIONAL PRACTICE

Statements of Ethical Principles
Adopted November 1991

The National Society of Fund Raising Executives exists to foster the development and growth of fund-raising professionals and the profession, to preserve and enhance philanthropy and volunteerism, and to promote high ethical standards in the fund-raising profession.

To these ends, this code declares the ethical values and standards of professional practice which NSFRE members embrace and which they strive to uphold in their responsibilities for generating philanthropic support.

Members of the National Society of Fund Raising Executives are motivated by an inner drive to improve the quality of life through the causes they serve. They seek to inspire others through their own sense of dedication and high purpose. They are committed to the improvement of their professional knowledge and skills in order that their performance will better serve others. They recognize their stewardship responsibility to ensure that needed resources are vigorously and ethically sought and that the intent of the donor is honestly fulfilled. Such individuals practice their profession with integrity, honesty, truthfulness and adherence to the absolute obligation to safeguard the public trust.

Furthermore, NSFRE members

- serve the ideal of philanthropy, are committed to the preservation and enhancement of volunteerism, and hold stewardship of these concepts as the overriding principle of professional life;
- put charitable mission above personal gain, accepting compensation by salary or set fee only;
- foster cultural diversity and pluralistic values and treat all people with dignity and respect;
- affirm, through personal giving, a commitment to philanthropy and its role in society;
- adhere to the spirit as well as the letter of all applicable laws and regulations;
- bring credit to the fund-raising profession by their public demeanor;
- recognize their individual boundaries of competence and are forthcoming about their professional qualifications and credentials;
- value the privacy, freedom of choice, and interests of all those affected by their actions;
- disclose all relationships which might constitute, or appear to constitute, conflicts of interest;
- actively encourage all their colleagues to embrace and practice these ethical principles;
- adhere to the following standards of professional practice in their responsibilities for generating philanthropic support.

Standards of Professional Practice
Adopted and incorporated into the NSFRE Code of Ethical Principles
November 1992

1. Members shall act according to the highest standards and visions of their institution, profession, and conscience.
2. Members shall avoid even the appearance of any criminal offense or professional misconduct.   *(continued)*

3. Members shall be responsible for advocating, within their own organizations, adherence to all applicable laws and regulations.

4. Members shall work for a salary or fee, not percentage-based compensation or a commission.

5. Members may accept performance-based compensation such as bonuses provided that such bonuses are in accord with prevailing practices within the member's own organizations and are not based on a percentage of philanthropic funds raised.

6. Members shall neither seek nor accept finder's fees and shall, to the best of their ability, discourage their organizations from paying such fees.

7. Members shall effectively disclose all conflicts of interest; such disclosure does not preclude or imply ethical impropriety.

8. Members shall accurately state their professional experience, qualifications, and expertise.

9. Members shall adhere to the principle that all donor and prospect information created by, or on behalf of, an institution is the property of that institution and shall not be transferred or utilized except on behalf of that institution.

10. Members shall, on a scheduled basis, give donors the opportunity to have their names removed from lists which are sold to, rented to, or exchanged with other organizations.

11. Members shall not disclose privileged information to unauthorized parties.

12. Members shall keep constituent information confidential.

13. Members shall take care to ensure that all solicitation materials are accurate and correctly reflect the organization's mission and use of solicited funds.

14. Members shall, to the best of their ability, ensure that contributions are used in accordance with donors' intentions.

15. Members shall ensure, to the best of their ability, proper stewardship of charitable contributions, including timely reporting on the use and management of funds and explicit consent by the donor before altering the conditions of a gift.

16. Members shall ensure, to the best of their ability, that donors receive informed and ethical advice about the value and tax implications of potential gifts.

17. Member's actions shall reflect concern for the interests and well-being of individuals affected by those actions. Members shall not exploit any relationship with a donor, prospect, volunteer, or employee to the benefit of the member or the member's organization.

18. In stating fund-raising results, members shall use accurate and consistent accounting methods that conform to the appropriate guidelines adopted by the American Institute of Certified Public Accountants (AICPA)* for the type of institution involved. (*In countries outside of the United States, comparable authority should be utilized.)

19. All of the above notwithstanding, members shall comply with all applicable local, state, provincial, and federal civil and criminal law.

Amended: March, 1993; October, 1994

SOURCE: *National Society of Fund Raising Executives. (1992; amended 1993, 1994).* NSFRE code of ethical principles and standards of professional practice. *Alexandria, VA: Author. Reprinted with permission.*

FIGURE 1-5. A DONOR BILL OF RIGHTS

A Donor
Bill *of* Rights

*P*hilanthropy is based on voluntary action for the common good. It is a tradition of giving and sharing that is primary to the quality of life. To assure that philanthropy merits the respect and trust of the general public, and that donors and prospective donors can have full confidence in the not-for-profit organizations and causes they are asked to support, we declare that all donors have these rights:

1. To be informed of the organization's mission, of the way the organization intends to use donated resources, and of its capacity to use donations effectively for their intended purposes.
2. To be informed of the identity of those serving on the organization's governing board, and to expect the board to exercise prudent judgment in its stewardship responsibilities.
3. To have access to the organization's most recent financial statements.
4. To be assured their gifts will be used for the purposes for which they were given.
5. To receive appropriate acknowledgment and recognition.
6. To be assured that information about their donations is handled with respect and with confidentiality to the extent provided by law.
7. To expect that all relationships with individuals representing organizations of interest to the donor will be professional in nature.
8. To be informed whether those seeking donations are volunteers, employees of the organization or hired solicitors.
9. To have the opportunity for their names to be deleted from mailing lists that an organization may intend to share.
10. To feel free to ask questions when making a donation and to receive prompt, truthful and forthright answers.

DEVELOPED BY: American Association of Fund-Raising Counsel (AAFRC), Association for Healthcare Philanthropy (AHP), Council for Advancement and Support of Education (CASE), National Society of Fund Raising Executives (NSFRE).

INITIAL ENDORSERS: Independent Sector, National Catholic Development Conference (NCDC), National Committee on Planned Giving (NCPG), National Council for Resource Development (NCRD), United Way of America.

SOURCE: *Kaplan, A. E. (Ed.). (1995). Giving USA—1995. New York: AAFRC Trust for Philanthropy. Reprinted with permission.*

REFERENCES

Broce, T. E. (1986). *Fund raising: The guide to raising money from private sources.* (2nd ed.). Norman: University of Oklahoma Press.

Gray, S., & Moore, J. (1996a, July 9). Big gifts from big business. *The Chronicle of Philanthropy, 7*(19), 1, 12–16, 18.

Gray, S., & Moore, J. (1996b, July 9). Corporate-giving departments turn to "outsourcing" to save money. *The Chronicle of Philanthropy, 7*(19), 18.

Hodgkinson, V. A., Weitzman, M. S., Noga, S. M., & Gorski, H. A. (1992). *Giving and volunteering in the United States: Findings from a national survey.* Washington, DC: Independent Sector.

Huntsinger, J. (1982). *Fund raising letters: A comprehensive study guide to raising money by direct response marketing.* Richmond, VA: Emerson.

Kaplan, A. E. (Ed.). (1993). *Giving USA—1993.* New York: AAFRC Trust for Philanthropy.

Kaplan, A. E. (Ed.). (1995). *Giving USA—1995.* New York: AAFRC Trust for Philanthropy.

Kaplan, A. E. (Ed.). (1996). *Giving USA—1996.* New York: AAFRC Trust for Philanthropy.

Meyers, R. S. (1989). *Financial management for nonprofit human service agencies.* Springfield, IL: Charles C Thomas.

Mixer, J. R. (1993). *Principles of professional fundraising: Useful foundations for successful practice.* San Francisco: Jossey-Bass.

National Charities Information Bureau. (1994, December). NCIB standards in philanthropy. *Wise Giving Guide,* p. 7.

National Society of Fund Raising Executives. (1992). NSFRE code of ethical principles and standards of professional practice. Alexandria, VA: Author.

Nichols, J. E. (1990, August). Philanthropic trends for the 1990s. *Fund Raising Management, 21*(6), 45–46.

Panas, J. (1984). *Megagifts: Who gives them, who gets them.* Chicago: Pluribus Press.

Panas, J. (1996, August). The sky is falling, the sky is falling: But don't worry, it could be philanthropy raining down. *Contributions, 10*(4), 1, 15–16, 19, 29, 31.

Schneiter, P. H. (1985). *The art of asking: How to solicit philanthropic gifts.* Amber, PA: Fund Raising Institute.

Sublett, D., & Stone, K. (1993). *The UCLA women and philanthropy focus groups, 1992.* Los Angeles: University of California Development Office.

CHAPTER 2

THE PROCESS OF FUNDRAISING

G iving is a personal thing, a dynamic and complicated process that is often emotional and prompted by an individual's personal life experience or association with an issue or organization. Nevertheless, a few important and time-tested truths exist in successful fundraising. Successful fundraising requires the highest commitment to integrity, responsiveness, and persistence. People give to people, and personal relationships are at the center of most successful fundraising activities. This is not to say that a strong belief in a certain cause, a sense of loyalty to an organization, civic pride, or the dozens of other possible factors that were discussed in chapter 1 do not play a role in motivating individuals to give. People consider many factors before parting with their resources.

A close relationship between the donor and the recipient, however, is at the core of most activities that typically lead to significant giving. This relationship is one that often is nurtured over months and years and involves several key events and individuals. Rarely does a significant gift occur as a result of a single act or invitation. Like meaningful friendships, successful donor relationships are nurtured over time with careful attention to individual needs and with a sincere interest in the well-being of the donor.

In this chapter, we discuss the profile of a successful fundraiser. We review methods to build a donor base, implement effective cultivation strategies that nurture such successful relationships, and track prospect activities. We address the important issue of organizational readiness and offer strategies to help your nonprofit put effective fundraising structures into place. We provide tips on developing an effective case for support and writing successful proposals. Using the broadly accepted gift pyramid, we consider the issue of setting realistic fundraising goals and discuss the importance of developing diverse and layered fundraising strategies that include both annual giving and major gift work. Finally, we offer creative ideas for donor acknowledgment and stewardship.

FUNDRAISERS WEAR MANY HATS

Individuals involved in fundraising for nonprofits must play multiple, and sometimes competing, roles. Part of their focus is external to, or outside of, their organizations, whereas another part relates to a range of issues that are internal. Some of what fundraisers do requires extraordinary flexibility. Other aspects of the job require more structured approaches with high degrees of organizational control. Turner (1995) compares the role of a fundraiser with that of an orchestra leader who

> is responsible for selecting the music, for arranging it or approving its arrangement, and for getting the best from the musicians and their instruments to appeal to the audience's aesthetic needs and desires. The fundraiser has a similar task and must orchestrate the following components: justifying "asking" for funds, mobilizing resources, planning and organizing, managing the "asking," and involving all appropriate parts of the community, including ethnic communities. (pp. 1039–1040)

Successful fundraisers must exhibit good leadership ability. The various roles performed by fundraisers are captured well by Quinn (1988), who identified the following basic categories or sets of skills that offer a framework for effective leadership: boundary spanning, human relations, coordinating, and directing skills. Figure 2-1 depicts the axes of flexibility versus control and internal versus external, as well as the four skill sets and various roles that fundraisers must play.

When using boundary-spanning skills, nonprofit fundraisers must be both brokers and innovators. They must serve as a bridge between their organization and a range of external constituencies by, among other things, ensuring that the nonprofit has a positive image in the commu-

FIGURE 2-1. COMPETING VALUES FRAMEWORK OF LEADERSHIP ROLES

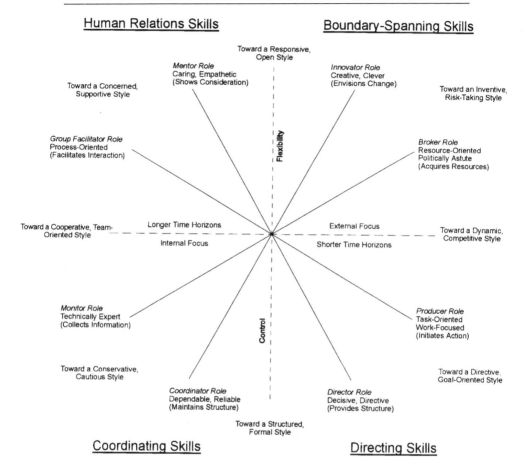

SOURCE: *Quinn, R. E. (1988). Beyond rational management: Mastering the paradoxes and competing demands of high performance. San Francisco: Jossey-Bass. Adapted with permission.*

nity and that its mission is clearly understood by others. Boundary spanning also involves developing relationships with a wide range of other organizations, including corporations and foundations. The performance of boundary-spanning skills requires a great deal of flexibility. To be effective, fundraisers must be visionary leaders able to engage in environmental scanning and capable of recognizing and taking advantage of spontaneous opportunities.

At the same time, they must adequately perform a range of skills that involve both monitoring and coordinating. They must put into place and ensure the smooth operation of important information and work management systems, including those that enable the organization to identify, research, and track prospects, as well as those that provide up-to-date information relative to time lines and goal attainment. There also must be systems that generate gift receipts that meet Internal Revenue Service (IRS) regulations, ensure that donors are appropriately thanked in a timely manner, and generate stewardship reports on a regular basis. In addition, fundraisers must maintain an accurate record-keeping system that stores information about pledges, planned gifts, and special events.

Successful fundraisers also must have skills that relate to both their own role as a producer of work and their role in directing the work of others. They must provide leadership in the development, implementation, and monitoring of strategic fundraising plans and establish ambitious yet realistic funding goals.

Finally, fundraising success requires highly developed human relations skills. Fundraisers must be caring and empathic mentors, they must show genuine concern for others, and they must be effective group facilitators tuned into the importance of process, involvement, and inclusiveness. In short, fundraisers must be "people oriented" and capable of developing meaningful personal relationships with board members, other volunteers, staff, and, most importantly, with prospective donors.

Fundraisers, like others who occupy positions of leadership, must be capable of playing numerous roles more or less simultaneously (Edwards & Austin, 1991) (Figure 2-1). They also must be able to successfully negotiate many issues in an environment of competing values and demands.

The challenging and demanding nature of fundraising is increasingly being recognized and rewarded in the nonprofit sector. A recent survey (Duronio, 1993) indicates that fundraisers are receiving high compensation for their work, with top salaries reported in the fields of education and health care followed by human services, the arts, and religion. Fundraisers report general satisfaction in their work and, in most cases, report a strong commitment to the organizations they represent as well as the profession. Most learned how to be fundraisers through on-the-job training, and most reported having worked in some other professional area before working in fundraising. Individuals with experience in "people professions" tend to be well-suited for careers in fundraising.

Many, if not most, nonprofits are unable to devote sufficient resources during the early stages of fundraising activities to hire full- or even part-time fundraising staff. Consequently, many nonprofit executives find that they and other senior staff must assume fundraising duties in addition to their normal management responsibilities. It can be done. However, given that the primary efforts of these individuals must be to "run the shop," the notion of wearing many hats and functioning in an environment of competing values takes on even greater significance.

DEVELOPING A DONOR BASE AND CULTIVATING DONOR RELATIONSHIPS

The fundraising process is a series of meaningful steps and interactions between the potential donor and the nonprofit organization that is often characterized as a spiral of five *i*'s: identification, information, interest, and involvement leading to investment (Worth, 1993) as shown in Figure 2-2.

The key to the fundraising process lies in building quality relationships with prospective donors. Cultivation of these relationships is the most important activity a nonprofit can undertake to achieve fundraising success. Identification is more than finding individuals in the community who have the resources to give. Finding such people is important, but more critical is determining whether those individuals are likely to give to your cause. This process of turning "suspects" into viable prospects can be done only through an adequate process of research and screening.

FIGURE 2-2. THE SPIRAL OF *I*'S IN SUCCESSFUL FUNDRAISING

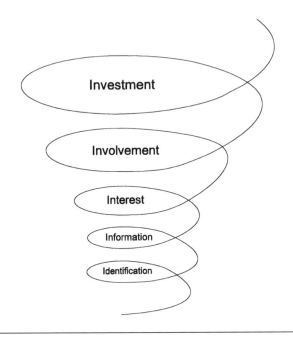

Methods for determining whether legitimate interest and potential to give exist are varied and range from word of mouth to sophisticated peer screening sessions and prospect software programs used by many colleges, universities, and large nonprofits. In any case, begin developing your prospect base by looking first at your "natural partners," that is, those individuals who have the closest association with your nonprofit. Typically, these individuals may include current and past clients and their families, board members, alumni, past donors, those who give to organizations with similar missions, and those who because of peer relationships may be receptive to considering a gift.

The concentric circle model, as shown in Figure 2-3, illustrates the process of identifying natural partners and other potential prospects. Place your nonprofit at the center of a circle and then draw several concentric rings around the center. Within each ring, identify prospect groups who have an established interest in your organization. Those groups with the closest association to your organization are represented in the inner circles. As you move outward from the center, the association becomes less significant. Your closest natural partners may not be the prospect group with the greatest resources. This is often the case for human services organizations. Figure 2-3 shows an example of this exercise for Genesis Home, an agency in Durham, North Carolina, that serves homeless families.

Giving potential for each of the groups representing a ring in the circle can be determined by seeking the input of peers, researching giving patterns, and keeping up with news on charitable giving through local newspapers and national publications such as *The Chronicle of Philanthropy*. Annual reports of private and corporate foundations and

FIGURE 2-3. NATURAL PARTNERS FOR GENESIS HOME

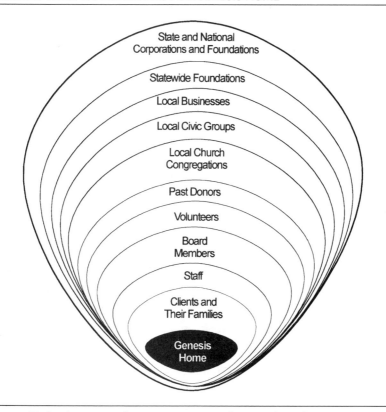

SOURCE: *Used with permission from Genesis Home, Durham, North Carolina.*

publications such as newsletters and annual reports from other nonprofit organizations are especially useful.

By far, the best information a nonprofit can collect on the giving potential of a group or individual will come from its own board members, staff, and volunteers. Informal meetings and phone inquiries may be sufficient to gather this information, or you may host small gatherings to "peer review" names of potential donors to determine capacity and generate information on prospects. You may then want to use alphabetical or numerical ratings to rank prospects by their potential giving levels and the likelihood of their giving at their capacity level. Of course, such information must always be handled with utmost confidentiality. In chapter 4 we explore the many methods available to gain useful information on your prospects and demonstrate how effective research on potential donors can lead to successful fundraising.

Turning suspects into viable donor prospects requires a thoughtful plan of activities to increase a prospect's involvement with your organization. These cultivation plans should be logically driven by what is known of the prospect's interests and giving potential. For example, high-level prospects should be engaged in ways that are more personal and involve your organization's top leadership.

Success in getting prospective donors to give at their capacity level will likely depend on how well your nonprofit develops and implements these plans and nurtures key relationships. Your goal should always be to bring about giving at the donor's level of capacity. You must adopt fundraising practices that place the potential donors and these key relationships at the center. Think again of a series of concentric circles of events and activities that happen in your nonprofit. In this case, place the donor at the center and begin to weave a plan of activities that takes place over time and that encourages meaningful involvement of the donor in the life of your organization. Figure 2-4 illustrates this activity for an arts organization.

Nonprofits must be creative in the ways that they cultivate potential donors. One key to successful cultivation is involving the prospect or donor in activities that are as close to the mission of your nonprofit

FIGURE 2-4. DONOR-CENTERED CULTIVATION CIRCLE

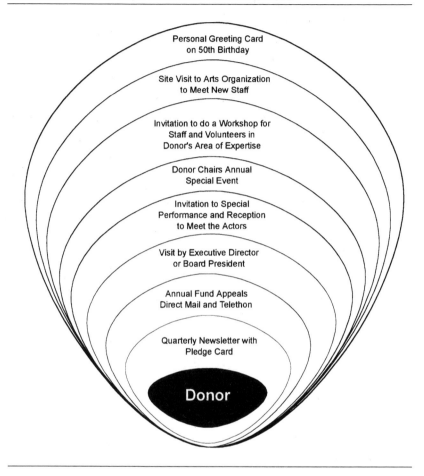

Personal Greeting Card
on 50th Birthday

Site Visit to Arts Organization
to Meet New Staff

Invitation to do a Workshop for
Staff and Volunteers in
Donor's Area of Expertise

Donor Chairs Annual
Special Event

Invitation to Special
Performance and Reception
to Meet the Actors

Visit by Executive Director
or Board President

Annual Fund Appeals
Direct Mail and Telethon

Quarterly Newsletter with
Pledge Card

Donor

as possible. Arrange for prospective donors to see your staff in action, provide them with varied opportunities to interact with staff and clients, or invite them to special functions or events. Homeless shelters or soup kitchens offer unique opportunities to share a meal. Arts organizations may have special children's programs or other events that would be appropriate for donor participation. Do not overlook daily activities that may seem uninteresting to you. What follows is a list of suggestions for cultivating your key prospects.

- Arrange a personal visit from the executive director or board president.
- Send a stewardship report on the impact of past giving.
- Seek advice from the prospect on his or her area of expertise.
- Involve the prospect in cultivating others.
- Honor the prospect with awards and special recognition.
- Send personal congratulations on birthdays, anniversaries, and promotions.
- Seek input on developing the case for support.
- Recruit the prospect to serve in a key role at a special event.
- Invite the prospect to do a workshop for staff.
- Invite the prospect to serve on a trustee or advisory board.
- Communicate regularly with annual reports, brochures, and speech reprints.
- Send frequent personal notes about items and events that interest the donor.

Managing the donor relationship means staying in touch with your prospective donors through phone calls, cards and notes, and personal visits. Note family birthdays and special dates and acknowledge job promotions and other important life events. Often, a newspaper article will provide such information. For high-level donors, monthly contact of some sort is a good rule.

Good prospect management requires that you take appropriate steps to identify potential donors, gather useful information about giving capacity, establish that a viable interest in your organization exists, and engage the prospect in meaningful involvement over time. This process is fundamental to your nonprofit's success in fundraising.

PROSPECT TRACKING

Failure to keep adequate records that document the events and milestones in the life of an organization is a common problem for nonprofits. This failure can result in lack of service continuity, poor transfer of knowledge, public relations nightmares, and loss of potential financial support.

Successful fundraising requires special attention to record keeping. Nonprofits must implement a system to document all prospect-related information, activities, and contacts. Such a system should be simple and user friendly. Although many software programs exist to help organizations manage donor information, two simple written forms and a good tickler system are adequate for most nonprofits.

The first form (Figure 2-5) should be a continually updated record of basic information about the prospect that includes home address and phone; family composition; work title, address, and phone; church affiliation; hobbies or special interests; and community service activities. The nature of the prospect's affiliation with your organization also is important, as well as information about such things as past giving to your nonprofit and others, estimated salary level and known assets, anticipated giving level, and a section to note such items as preferred method of contact and important peer relationships. Be sure to date each entry and indicate the source of your information (for example, a newspaper clipping, corporate annual report, or information from a peer). This form can be altered slightly to include such items as application deadlines and proposal submission information to be used for foundation and corporate prospects.

The second essential form is used for recording or tracking contacts with a prospect or donor (Figure 2-6). Include such information as the type of contact and participants, subject of discussion or purpose for contact, outcome of contact, and next steps. Note when cards are sent or phone contacts made. Keep a paper file of all original correspondence received and copies of everything sent to the donor. A simple tickler system will ensure that you remember such things as birthdays, special events, and proposal deadlines. All information on prospects and donors should be handled and stored with great attention to confidentiality. As discussed in chapter 1, ensuring donors confidentiality in their giving activities is an important ethical requirement in fundraising. If written information about specific prospects or donors is provided for the purposes of a board meeting or volunteer function, all copies should be collected at the close of the meeting.

FIGURE 2-5. PROSPECT BIOGRAPHICAL FORM

Prospect's Full Name _____

Home Address (City, State, Zip) _____

Business Title _____

Business Address _____

Home Phone _____   Work Phone _____
Business Title _____   Occupation _____
Date of Birth _____   Nickname _____
Marital Status ❑ Married   ❑ Divorced   ❑ Single
Spouse's Name _____

Spouse's Occupation _____   Date of Birth _____
Religious Affiliation _____   Hobbies _____
Professional Affiliations _____

Education   (Name)   (Course/Degree)   (Year)
_____

Children   (Name)   (Sex)   (Date of Birth)   (Notes)
_____

_____

Est. Annual Income $ _____   Est. Net Worth $ _____

         Recent Gifts   Other Org. Gifts
    (Year/Amount/Purpose)   (Year/Amount/Purpose)
    _____   _____

    _____   _____

    _____   _____

    _____   _____

Association with Organization
_____

_____

_____

FIGURE 2-6. PROSPECT TRACKING FORM

Person Making Contact _____   Date of Contact _____

I. Prospect Identification
    Name _____
    Address _____
    City, State _____

II. Summary of Contact
    Date of Contact _____
    Purpose _____
    Results of Contact _____

III. Ask Amount
    Anticipated Gift Level _____
    Gift Outlook _____

IV. Next Step
    Date of Future Contact _____
    Purpose _____
    Summary _____

V. New Information Gathered (interests, other charities, individuals
    mentioned, or biographical information)

    _____
    _____
    _____
    _____
    _____
    _____
    _____
    _____
    _____

PREPARING YOUR ORGANIZATION TO RAISE FUNDS

Balancing the needs and interests of donors with those of your non-profit is not easy and requires the commitment of your top staff and volunteer leadership. The old adage "it takes money to raise money" is true. Developing a strong fundraising program also takes a great deal of time and energy. A nonprofit may spend as much as 50 cents of every dollar raised to support the staff time and activities needed to raise that money; many nonprofits discover that they spend much more. Aim to keep your fundraising expenses to approximately 25 cents or less for each dollar raised. Of course, if a large amount of money is raised, the percentage of expenses, or the costs of raising the money, will typically be a good deal lower than when smaller amounts are raised. In addition, the cost of raising money during the early phases of an organization's fundraising efforts is likely to be higher than during later phases.

Every organization is unique in the amount of time and resources needed to raise funds. Many organizations will allocate a percentage of a staff person's time to raise money; others will hire full- or part-time development professionals. Regardless, the key to fundraising success is that your nonprofit make a clear commitment of staff time and resources for a sufficient period. Our experience suggests that you typically should plan to devote a minimum of three years to build a strong fundraising foundation.

Although fundraising activities may depend heavily on volunteer involvement, staff time must be clearly allocated for this purpose. A common mistake that nonprofits make is not providing sufficient staff support and oversight. This situation can quickly lead to volunteer burnout and public relations problems. Volunteers, particularly board members, are often eager to help with fundraising but may lack the knowledge and skills necessary to carry out the tasks involved. Nonprofits need a "point person" who has the big picture in mind at all times, can readily respond to volunteers' questions, and can promptly provide material and other types of support. Your nonprofit's top leadership must take responsibility for either assuming or overseeing this role. In many cases, potential donors (especially high-level donors and corporate and foundation staff members) will prefer to deal only with the executive director or board president. The involvement of your chief executive officer, board president, or both, lends great credibility and has a positive impact on the level of support a prospect may consider.

Activities that center on your relationships with donors will not only bring about meaningful and substantial giving but also will help your nonprofit develop a culture that encourages ongoing and positive staff and volunteer participation in fundraising activities. Such a culture can easily be detected by potential donors and is enormously important in establishing patterns of habitual giving.

More than 44 percent of all U.S. charitable dollars are given to support religious organizations (Kaplan, 1996). Churches, in particular, do an excellent job creating a positive culture of giving. A number of factors contributes to their success. Most importantly, churches *ask*, and they do so on a regular basis. In religious institutions, giving is expected *and* highly valued (Klein, 1994). Churches also tend to be good stewards of people's money, and typically they use excellent follow-up techniques.

LAUNCHING A FUNDRAISING CAMPAIGN

Several important readiness factors should be considered before launching an organized fundraising program or campaign. First, assess your internal readiness by addressing the extent to which your current board composition is adequate to support fundraising. The importance of recruiting and retaining strong and active board members cannot be overstated. At no time is the strength of a nonprofit board more important than when launching a fundraising campaign. Consider the following to ensure that your board is structured for effective fundraising:

+ Recruit at least one attorney and one accountant to your board to provide guidance on charitable tax law issues, deferred giving, and the appropriate handling of gifts other than cash, such as securities and property.

- Be sure that your board includes at least one representative from the local business community.
- If possible, recruit at least one "famous" individual to your board (for example, someone who is highly recognizable and widely esteemed, such as a top-level business executive, local television or radio personality, or athlete).
- Be certain that you have several "worker bees" on your board, individuals who are willing to do the hard, and sometimes not so glamorous, work of fundraising, such as making phone calls and visits, hosting gatherings, and stuffing envelopes.
- If possible, recruit at least a few individuals to your board who have wealth, can identify a peer group of other wealthy individuals whom they would be willing to contact, and who would be willing to go "public" with their giving.
- Include on your board someone connected to the print or broadcast media, such as a reporter or feature writer, or someone strong in public relations.
- Make sure your board is reflective of the community you serve in terms of such characteristics as gender, race, ethnicity, and socioeconomic status.

The second step in preparing your organization to raise funds is putting in place a leadership structure that extends beyond your board to support fundraising activities. This preparation may involve establishing a time-limited subcommittee of your board or a special fundraising steering committee made up of those individuals willing to take on the responsibility of fundraising. This committee should be relatively small (eight to 10 members) and represent the geographic, cultural, and economic diversity of your prospect base. Members of this group must be available, flexible, and knowledgeable about your organization and the communities they represent. They also must be willing to do the hard work of fundraising, such as making prospect calls, stuffing envelopes, and participating in all aspects of planning and implementation. In essence, members of this committee are your worker bees.

You also should consider creating what is sometimes called an "advisory council." Members of this group will typically have a close association with your major gift prospects or, ideally, represent your major prospects' peer group. Advisory council members will often be high-level business and community leaders who perhaps have little knowledge of your organization but are willing to offer their endorsement and, most important, help you gain access to major gift prospects. Some of these individuals may be willing to serve in "name only" to enhance your nonprofit's visibility and credibility. Others may be willing to sign a document indicating their support, co-chair a special event, or sign a solicitation letter. Still others may offer valuable information about potential funders, accompany staff or volunteers on prospect visits, make phone calls of endorsement, or open doors to otherwise inaccessible funding sources. Look for individuals who have a close association with your top prospect pool.

Figure 2-7 illustrates the type of organizational structure that will effectively support a major fundraising campaign. As the figure shows, when you think about establishing structures to support your fundraising efforts, place the donor in the center. This placement helps to reinforce the importance of the donor relationship visually and functionally. From the center, or the donor, your organizational structure includes an advisory council, fundraising steering committee, board of trustees, and the development officer or executive director.

Before launching a fundraising program, your staff and board members must clearly understand the resource needs of the organization and agree on funding strategies. Nothing is more destructive than confusing the public and potential prospects with mixed messages, poorly-thought-out strategies, or botched attempts. You should invest time up front with board members and staff in a process of internal assessment and planning to ensure clarity concerning goals and procedures. Such a process should review closely your nonprofit's mission statement, its funding needs, the impact that increased funds will enable you to make in the community, the strategies and necessary budget for fundraising activities, and the personnel needed to carry out these activities.

Figure 2-8 may be a useful tool in determining whether your nonprofit is ready to embark on a fundraising campaign (Read, 1986). Your staff, board members, and other key volunteers should participate in

FIGURE 2-7. ORGANIZATIONAL STRUCTURE TO SUPPORT A FUNDRAISING CAMPAIGN

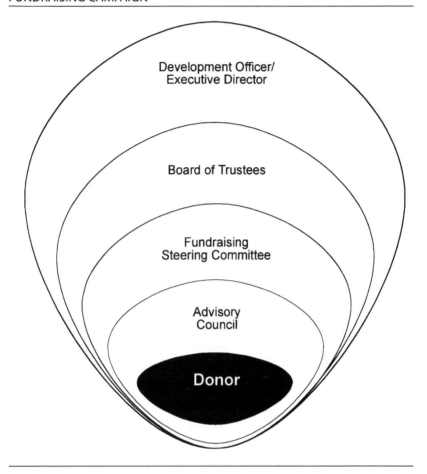

responding to such questions to determine common ground or discover areas of disagreement.

Next, consider your external readiness by addressing the following questions:

- What is the current climate of giving in your community?
- What other organizations are in the midst of a campaign?
- Will perceptions of the state of the economy affect your efforts?
- Is your prospect pool adequate to support your needs?
- Are you ready to go public with your needs and strategies?

FIGURE 2-8. ASSESSING YOUR ORGANIZATIONAL READINESS FOR FUNDRAISING

1. Is your organization structured to receive foundation or corporate support? (Note date of Internal Revenue Service ruling or agreement with qualified sponsoring organization.)

_____

_____

2. What is the central purpose of the activity for which you are seeking funding?

_____

_____

   (a)   What is the *subject* focus of the activity?

_____

_____

   (b)   What *geographic* area will be served by the activity? Will this project have an impact beyond the geographic area?

_____

_____

   (c)   What population groups will benefit from this activity?

_____

_____

3. How does this activity fit into the central purpose of your organization?

_____

_____

(continued)

4. What are the unique qualifications of staff members to accomplish the
proposed activity?

_____

_____

5. What is the total budget for the project?

(a)   What type of support (for example, building funds, equipment,
operating support, and so forth) are you seeking?

_____

_____

(b)   How much grant support are you seeking?

_____

(c)   What other sources of support will be used to meet the project
costs?

_____

(d)   How will the project be funded for the long term?

_____

6. Who has supported or expressed an interest in your organization's
programs? (Note past and current funders, members of the board of
directors, volunteers, community leaders.)

_____

_____

SOURCE: *Adapted from Read, P. E. (Ed.). (1986). Foundation fundamentals: A guide
for grantseekers (3rd ed.). Copyright © 1986 by The Foundation Center, 79 Fifth
Avenue, New York, NY 10003. Used with permission.*

Sometimes organizations can "ride the wave" of a hot public issue or be swamped by it. The national publicity surrounding the O. J. Simpson trial served to increase public awareness of and giving to programs that address domestic violence. However, the public scandal involving William Aramony, the former chief executive officer of United Way of America, had a devastating effect on giving to United Ways across the country (Dundjerski, 1995).

External readiness is difficult to determine, and we are always in a dynamic environment to raise funds. However, a proactive, informed posture can prevent your nonprofit from being devastated by an unexpected environmental or economic occurrence.

MAKING THE CASE FOR SUPPORT

Perhaps the most important tool in a successful fundraising program is your nonprofit's case for support. The case statement differs from a mission statement in that the case for support documents the funding needs of your nonprofit and makes the case for why your organization should be supported. The case statement is typically less broad than a mission statement and is time-limited as a result of its specificity regarding funding needs.

The case statement should be short (one to three pages) and written in language laypeople can understand. It should complement other organization materials but serve to specifically support your fundraising efforts. Seymour (1988), who is often regarded as a pioneer in fundraising, states that a case statement "should aim high, provide perspective, arouse a sense of history and continuity, convey a feeling of importance, relevance and urgency, and have whatever stuff is needed to warm the heart and stir the mind" (p. 43).

As Seymour indicates, the case for support is more than a funding appeal. It should tell a story, illustrate how your nonprofit is responding to a particular community need, and clearly explain why financial support from donors is critically important at this time. When developing your case for support, keep in mind the following essential elements:

- Make it concise, compelling, and clear.
- Keep it simple.
- Describe the need for both the services and the funds.
- Provide supporting data.
- Present credentials and successes.
- State the funding goal.

A case statement is not designed to stand alone but is best used as a warm-up to a prospect visit or a leave-behind piece. It can be mailed with annual appeals or serve as a key campaign document.

When developing a case statement, try to avoid these common mistakes:

- too institutional
- too little rationale in terms of importance and urgency
- too little basis for confidence in organization
- too much catering to colleagues instead of audience
- too much emphasis on need rather than opportunity.

Human services agencies often make the mistake of thinking that if they can make a strong case for the service *need*, funding will naturally follow. Giving is an emotional issue, and individuals sometimes do respond to emotion-laden appeals. However, you can run into problems if you emphasize *need* over *opportunity*. Donors, particularly those who make high-level gifts, want to feel confident that their money will be used or invested wisely. They need to be assured of your nonprofit's credibility and long-term stability. Donors want to bet on the "winning horse," not invest in a losing operation. If your nonprofit is at risk of closing its doors because of inadequate funding, a one-time special appeal can be effective. However, basing your annual appeal or a sizable campaign on a message of desperation is not wise.

Case statements do not need to be multicolored, expensive publications. As was indicated in chapter 1, campaign literature has never been shown to be a strong giving motivator. A document that is simple but professional looking and that is done in-house is often adequate. In fact, a slick piece can send the wrong message about your nonprofit's needs. Keep it simple and low-budget with a strong emphasis on opportunity and credibility. Figures 2-9 and 2-10 are examples of case statements.

GOAL SETTING AND THE GIFT PYRAMID

An important step in launching your fundraising campaign is determining a funding goal that is ambitious yet realistic. Begin the process of determining such a goal by involving your key board members, staff, and volunteers in a fantasy exercise. Imagine what your nonprofit could do if resources were unlimited. Put a dollar value to this fantasy list and work from there. Next, begin to subject your list to a reality check, deciding which items are essential and which are long term and less critical. Then determine the feasibility of raising the funds needed to cover the items on your list by considering the following questions:

+ How much, if any, money has been raised in the past?
+ Can your current donor pool, if you have one, support such a goal?
+ Do you need operating, program, capital, or endowment funds?
+ What does your internal and external readiness assessment suggest in terms of a goal?
+ Do you need resources to maintain the current level of service or are you seeking to expand?
+ In the current social and political environment, how "sellable" are your needs?
+ Can your current leadership structure, both staff and volunteer, support such a goal?
+ How much money have other organizations with a similar mission and makeup raised in your community?

The work you have done in assessing your nonprofit's internal and external readiness will be of great help in determining a feasible goal. Timing is often critical, so be directed by this sense of organizational readiness and stay tuned to local and national events and issues that may have an impact on your fundraising results.

FIGURE 2-9. SAMPLE CASE STATEMENT

Volunteers for Youth

The children are our future.

We must give our children a chance to grow up healthy and safe. They need positive adult role models who can guide them, give them advice and teach them how to succeed in the modern world.

However, our children are too often being left at home alone while their parents struggle to make ends meet. Many of their "role models" are selling or using drugs, and violence is a part of everyday life.

Children in North Carolina fared worse this year than they did a year ago in many ways. According to the Children's Index, published by the Child Advocacy Institute, juvenile arrests rose 6.5%, the number of children living in poverty rose 8.7% and the high school dropout rate rose 9.5%.

We believe in a brighter future—but we need YOUR help.

OUR MISSION

Volunteers for Youth has provided positive role models to the youth of Orange County for the past 14 years. The organization was founded in 1982 by several members of our community.

You can see the difference we make in Orange County: an adult spending the day at the library with a child; a member of the community supervising a teenager completing court-ordered community service; college students spending their spare time every week working with middle school children after school. These are just some of the ways adults can make a difference in the lives of children.

Most of the services we provide could not exist without the help of adult volunteers from the community. In 1995, approximately 100 volunteers helped us make a difference in the lives of 165 children from all over Orange County.

However, our one-on-one program, in which an adult spends four hours a week with a young friend for one year, desperately needs more volunteers. Because we lack the resources to recruit a sufficient number of volunteers, some children have to wait at least six months, and others never get matched. This must change.

HOW YOU CAN HELP

We are seeking funds for the following projects to improve the services we offer to the children in our community:

- $20,000 for the development of the position of recruitment and retention specialist. Outcome: No child in Orange County will have to wait more than one month for a volunteer.
- $5,000 to expand our after-school program. Outcome: All middle school children in Orange County will have an opportunity to spend time after school with positive adult role models from the community.

We also appreciate in-kind donations. Can you help our children get discounts or passes to special events? Do you have the spare time to volunteer to make a difference in one child's life?

NOTE: *This case statement was developed by Myrna A. Miller and is reprinted with permission.*

FIGURE 2-10. SAMPLE CASE STATEMENT

KEY Players

Today's youth are faced with ever more complex problems and issues. Violence and drug use among youth are on the rise. In 1994, 6,937 criminal incidents were reported to the N.C. Board of Education, and 17,000 students were suspended for assault and battery on another student. The numbers of reported arrests of young people—children younger than 14—for violent offenses increased by 100% in 1994.*

Unfortunately, our children often face these and other problems and issues with ever-decreasing resources from which they can draw positive responses. There is a tremendous need for prevention and education to create a healthy, positive school environment. KEY Players was established to speak to the concerns of today's youth.

Even our names speaks volumes—KEY is an acronym for Keep Empowering Youth. This 501(c)(3) not-for-profit professional theatre company was formed five years ago to serve K–12 school children and educators throughout the state by enhancing the classroom experience through theatrical events, workshops, and reinforcement materials that can be integrated into the curriculum.

Our Mission

Our mission is to provide issue-oriented theatrical experiences that equip all youth to make positive choices in their lives. We believe that this results from understanding alternatives, realizing consequences and believing in the individual self. We work to help children in the audience find within themselves the critical reasoning needed to make positive decisions to improve their lives and better their situations.

KEY's professional, adult actor/educators perform plays and lead educational workshops for children, young adults, educators and others throughout North Carolina.

Our Approach

Our instructive theatre is unique. We use principles of theatre, psychology and education to change the thinking and behavior of our audiences. And it's interactive—actors and the audience actually talk with each other. We're one of only two theatre companies in the nation applying these valued techniques in schools. The plays are fun and educational. This year's programs include

+ *Ouch!* and *Owie!* teach why violence hurts.
+ *Expect Respect!* addresses harassment and respect for self and others.
(*Statistics from the N.C. Dept. of Public Instruction)

(continued)

FIGURE 2-10. SAMPLE CASE STATEMENT *(continued)*

+ *No Way!* provides children with practical refusal skills.
+ *Trash!* teaches respect for the environment and recycling.

KEY's instructive programs have been recognized for their contributions: Outstanding Public Awareness Program by the N.C. Association of County Commissioners, and Outstanding Educational Program by the N.C. Recycling Association.

In five short years we've reached 80,000 kids in 22 counties in over 500 events. Everywhere we go, we're asked to come back.

Our Needs

To serve all schools, KEY actively seeks alternate methods of funding to supplement or fully pay for performances in school systems through the private sector, government agencies, grants and gifts.

We also offer the value of crossing over from "theatre in the schools" to issues-oriented theatre that serves multiple purposes and is often funded from budgets other than performing arts.

To continue our mission of empowering today's youth, we count on the support and resources of generous contributors throughout the state and even beyond our borders. We've identified critical areas requiring support:

+ *Scholarship Fund:* Underwrite programs for schools that have inadequate resources. Funding for schools is decided on a case-by-case basis, based on needs criteria and a school's willingness to make it happen.
+ *Equipment Fund:* We're in need of several items, including a 15-passenger van to transport actors, sets and props; TV, VCR, and video recorder.
+ *Housing Fund:* We're in search of housing for our company of actor/ educators during each school year.
+ *Endowment Fund:* Our long-term goal of a $1 million endowment is an investment in the future. It will ensure staff salaries for our three full-time employees: executive director, artistic director and managing director.
+ *General Operating Support:* $100,000 for operations of our office and keeping the acting company on the road and in our schools.

We'll be happy to provide any additional information you need. Please call us.

NOTE: *This case statement was developed by Lois A. Boynton. Reprinted with permission.*

By far, the most useful tool in determining a feasible goal is the gift pyramid. The gift pyramid is based on the widely accepted rule of thirds that suggests that at least one-third, and often close to one-half, of your goal will come from your top 10 to 15 gifts, the second third of your goal will come from the next 25 or so gifts, and the remaining third will come from all other gifts. In recent years, many experts have suggested that we place an even stronger emphasis on top gift levels and follow an 80–20 formula. This formula suggests that 80 percent of your goal will come from your top 20 gifts.

Whether you follow the rule of thirds or the 80–20 formula, the important issue is the value and emphasis you place on securing leadership gifts. It has been shown that simple "numbers" reasoning (that is, if we can just get 1,000 people to each give $100) does not work. This approach flattens your overall giving, thus depressing your true giving potential, and falsely assumes that a single strategy or gift level will successfully appeal to all your donors. Instead, in successful fundraising campaigns, goals are met by carefully determining donor capacity, developing diverse strategies that match that capacity, and focusing heavily on donor activities that will produce the largest gifts.

Figure 2-11 shows what a gift pyramid with a goal of $50,000 would look like, using the rule of thirds.

Gift pyramids are most useful for time-limited campaigns in which your nonprofit is seeking to raise an unprecedented amount of money. If you are not able to identify prospects that have both the capacity and the likelihood to give at their rated level, your goal is probably not achievable. However, if you can meet the goal of your top one-third, you are likely to be successful.

Gift pyramids remind us that our time and energy should be spent cultivating top prospects and are useful in determining an appropriate time line for fundraising strategies. Always spend the early phase of a campaign cultivating and closing those leadership gifts. Go public with a campaign only after you have reached approximately 50 percent of your goal. Often known as the "quiet phase," the early months of a campaign

FIGURE 2-11. GIVING PYRAMID FOR $50,000 GOAL BASED ON THE RULE OF THIRDS

	Gift Level	Gifts Needed	Prospects Needed	Total Dollars
Top Third	5,000	2	6	10,000
	2,500	3	9	7,500
	1,000	5	15	5,000
				22,500
Middle Third	75	9	27	6,750
	500	12	36	6,000
	250	15	45	3,750
				16,500
Bottom Third	100	75	numerous	7,500
	gifts below	numerous		3,500
	100			11,000
			Grand Total	$50,000

NOTE: "Rule of thirds": It is generally true that at least one-third of your goal, and in many cases, up to one-half, will come from your top 10 to 15 gifts; the second third of your goal will come from the next 25 gifts or so; and the remaining third will come from all other gifts. NOTE: The number of prospects needed is based on the widespread belief that about one out of three prospects will make a gift at their capacity level if they have been appropriately cultivated and asked.

should be dedicated almost exclusively to cultivating and soliciting the relatively small group of your prospects who will enable you to reach one-third or more of your goal.

DEVELOPING DIVERSE AND LAYERED FUNDRAISING STRATEGIES

The strength of an organization's fundraising program can be measured in part by the diversity of its strategies. To what degree are your fundraising strategies tailored to the unique characteristics of a donor group? Are you successfully cultivating major donors while maintaining a strong annual income?

Many nonprofits make the mistake of relying on a single strategy—most typically, direct mail appeals or special events—to meet their funding objectives. Successful fundraising that builds a strong foundation for your nonprofit requires that multiple activities take place within a 12-month period, ideally including both annual giving activities and major gift work. These efforts should be carefully coordinated with the production of communication pieces such as newsletters. Your fundraising strategies also can be strengthened by partnering your efforts with community activities such as the opening of a new community playground or an annual street fair. Because most foundations have specific proposal submission deadlines, you often need to adjust your fundraising plans to accommodate these dates.

A good fundraising program should help you accomplish the following goals:

+ maintain a strong base of annual donors
+ steadily increase the giving level of annual donors
+ regularly bring in new donors
+ maintain active cultivation of major gift donors
+ make regular asks
+ promote a positive public image of your organization.

Be sure to take advantage of opportunities in the media to inform the public about the good work your nonprofit is doing. Good news coverage of a special event or success story can be a great boost to your fundraising efforts.

Annual Fund Strategies

Annual fund appeals typically bring in low-level but numerous gifts. The importance of such appeals is that they serve to establish a firm donor base, bring in somewhat predictable annual income, and encourage habitual giving. Annual gifts typically result from a letter or phone call prompted by a single event or activity. They are usually given in cash from current income, have short-term benefit, and are usually unrestricted.

Mail appeals are by far the most common method used by nonprofits to secure annual gifts. Klein (1994) suggests that "direct mail remains the least expensive way an organization can reach the most people with a message they can hold in their hands and examine at their leisure" (p. 58).

Typically, mail appeals generate small gifts, often ranging from $5 to $50. The response rates for mail solicitations vary greatly, ranging from 1 to 66 percent or more and are closely tied to the degree to which the recipient is already knowledgeable about and involved with your nonprofit (Klein, 1994). Mailings to past donors and individuals closely associated with your nonprofit, such as board members and volunteers, will typically produce much higher response rates than mailings to lapsed donors or "cold" prospects.

There are two principal functions of a direct mail solicitation: acquiring donors and retaining them. Donors are acquired by sending appeals to individuals who have not previously given to your nonprofit. The best results will be realized when you are able to compile mailing lists of prospects you have some reason to believe may have interest in or sympathy for your organization or cause. A response rate of 1 percent is not uncommon for this type of cold mailing, so your list must be fairly large for you to be successful in at least recovering your costs.

Most experts suggest that before mailing to a large list, you should conduct a test mailing to a sample of about 2,000 individuals (Klein, 1994). If your test mailing generates a response rate of 1 percent or more, then you can be confident that you are on track and should proceed with the remaining names. Remember that your primary goal for this type of mailing is to acquire new donors, so be satisfied with low gift levels. If you raise only enough money to cover your expenses, the appeal should be considered worthwhile. Once donors are acquired, you can begin to cultivate them, bringing them closer to your organization and, hopefully, closer to major gift support. You can expect some annual attrition of donors, so you should continually add new names to your mailing and invitation lists.

Once someone becomes a donor to your nonprofit, you need to be concerned about retention. You need to implement strategies to ensure that the individual remains loyal to your nonprofit and continues to give on a regular basis. You must develop cultivation strategies that enable you to have increasingly close contact with the donor.

A tried and true way to retain donors is to ask them for a gift more than once a year (Klein, 1994). Generally, you will want to ask most of your donors for a gift two or three times a year. The solicitation may be through a mail appeal, a telephone appeal, or a special event. Experience has shown that this frequency of asking does not offend people. Rather, it keeps your nonprofit's name in the donor's mind and enables you to take advantage of the ups and downs of donors' cash flows. Mail solicitations to past donors will typically generate a response rate of about 10 percent (Klein, 1994).

Seltzer (1987) offered the formula shown in Figure 2-12 to determine whether your direct mail campaign is a success.

Compared with direct mail appeals, telephone solicitations produce higher participation rates, often reaching 25 percent to 50 percent or more. One useful strategy is to select from among your direct mail donors those who have given above a certain level to be solicited by telephone. Members of your board or other volunteers can be asked to make the telephone calls during one or two evenings, after you have provided them with training on telephone solicitation and with dinner or refreshments. Make it a fun, party-like event with the goals of retaining each of your past donors and raising the level of their gifts. You may be pleasantly surprised at the results, particularly if you have sent each of your donors a warm-up letter alerting them to your upcoming call and thanking them in advance for their support.

Fundraising strategies, particularly annual fund activities such as direct mail, telethons, membership drives, and special events, should take into consideration typical giving patterns in a calendar year. Peaks and valleys exist in response rates to direct mail appeals. Many donors wait until the end of the calendar year to make their gifts. Others, if asked, will give several times throughout the year.

FIGURE 2-12. HOW TO DETERMINE WHETHER A DIRECT MAIL CAMPAIGN IS PROFITABLE

Ultimately, profitability is measured by income minus expenses. But there are other critical indices in assessing the success of a direct mail appeal.

1. **Response Rate.** The number of letters mailed relative to the number of contributions received is called the response rate. For example, if you mail out 1,000 letter appeals and receive 55 contributions in response, your response rate is 55 ÷ 1,000, which is 5.5 percent.

2. **Average Gift Size.** The size of the "average" contribution or gift is calculated by the total dollars raised divided by the number of contributions. For example, if you received $825 from 55 donors, the "average" gift would be $15.00 (825 ÷ 55).

   The response rate and average gift size are important in computing your profitability. By determining each of them, you can compare the results of different mailings in an objective and easy manner.

3. **The Average Cost.** The average cost of obtaining this response or contribution is determined by dividing the total cost of the mailing by the number of positive responses received. For example, if you mail out 1,000 letters at a total cost of $330.00, netting 55 positive responses, the average cost is $6.00 (330 ÷ 55). The cost of obtaining one contributor is $6.00.

4. By computing your average gift size and the average cost, you can figure out how much you spent on the average to raise your average gift. Using our example, the average gift is $15.00 and the average cost is $6.00. Each contribution of $15.00 cost you $6.00, yielding an average net contribution (or profit) of $9.00.

Source: Seltzer, M. (1987). Securing your organization's future: A complete guide to fundraising strategies. Copyright © 1987 by Michael Seltzer. Published by The Foundation Center, 79 Fifth Avenue, New York, NY 10003. Reprinted with permission.

Matching gifts (contributions made by a donor's employer) are a wonderful way to increase your overall level of support. Alert your donors to matching gift opportunities by including matching gift information on pledge cards and in your nonprofit's newsletter. Remember that matching gifts often come from a spouse's employer. To get a complete listing of companies who match employee gifts, write to Director, National Clearinghouse for Corporate Matching Gift Information, Council for Advancement and Support of Education, Suite 400, 11 Dupont Circle, NW, Washington, DC 20036-1261.

Finally, regularly include a pledge card in your nonprofit's newsletters and other publications. A pledge card will encourage giving and help to enhance your nonprofit's giving culture.

Major Gift Work

Typically, larger gifts will come about only if annual fund activities are complemented with major gift cultivation and solicitation. In contrast to annual gifts, major gifts typically are designated for a particular project. They are often a one-time commitment of an individual's assets rather than income and are usually made with much consideration of a donor's financial situation, including consideration of charitable tax benefits.

Successful major gift work requires intensive and personal contacts with potential donors over time, often several years. Similar to adhering to the spiral of the five *i*'s discussed earlier in this chapter, the following strategic seven-step process is important in securing major gift commitments:

1. Identify your prospects.
2. Qualify or rate your prospects.
3. Determine a cultivation strategy.
4. Meaningfully involve the prospect with your nonprofit.
5. Solicit the gift.
6. Close the gift and handle objections.
7. Acknowledge the gift and provide appropriate recognition or stewardship.

Identifying major gift prospects through effective networking and research has been discussed in this chapter and is considered more fully in chapter 4. The process of qualifying (that is, moving potential donors from the category of suspects to that of viable prospects) comes after identifying prospects. In addition to establishing that an interest and giving intent exists, an important part of the qualification process is determining the level of gift that you should seek (see chapter 4).

Developing and implementing a highly personalized cultivation strategy or plan that focuses on the prospect's involvement with your nonprofit is a vital component of major gift fundraising. This plan will bring together in meaningful ways potential donors and high-level staff and volunteers and often results in long-term mutually beneficial relationships. To put together creative and successful major gift cultivation plans, refer to the list of quality cultivation ideas presented earlier in this chapter. As you develop cultivation plans that lead to successful major gift fundraising, keep in mind the following concepts (Wood, 1991):

+ Know what is needed to take the next step.
+ Remember that prospects are people.
+ Know where you are and where you are going.
+ Find out what the donor needs and show him or her how to get it.
+ Manage objections into opportunities.
+ Remember that no isn't "no!" until it has been qualified.

Ideally, your cultivation plans will be constructed so carefully that you and your prospects will always know what comes next. Before ending a visit with a potential donor, discuss what follow-up steps are needed and agree on a clear time line. Make a special effort to learn about your prospects' work and home demands and be respectful of time constraints and day-to-day stresses. Your nonprofit may become an important priority for a prospect, although getting to that point may take time. Each prospect is an individual who is likely to have many demands on his or her time and resources. We find it useful to ask a potential donor directly which organizations rank as her or his top charitable priorities. Ask prospects what needs to take place for them to rank *your* organization near or at the top.

The Major Gift Ask

If your cultivation plans are effective and successful, making the ask often can be easy. In major gift fundraising, it is usually important to ask for a specific amount for a specific program or need. Sometimes, you can start with a gift range and a couple of program options, but if you are truly ready to make the ask (capacity, intent, interest, and involvement are determined and established), it is often better to ask a major gift donor for a specific amount.

The major gift ask is typically done by the staff member or volunteer with the closest relationship to the donor, but often involvement by a peer or high-level staff or board member is essential. With individual major gift prospects, the ask is almost always done face-to-face with a supplementary written proposal available. Corporate and foundation asks will vary widely according to proposal guidelines and typically rely on written requests.

Because many major gifts come in the form of a pledge that is paid over years, a pledge letter or letter of intent with a blank space for a signature, gift amount, and pay out wishes may be useful when soliciting a major gift prospect. If possible, close the gift during your face-to-face meeting, that is, get the commitment in writing on the day of the solicitation. If a written commitment is not possible at that time, a pledge letter sent immediately after your visit may suffice. Figure 2-13 is an example of a pledge letter.

Handling Objections

What do you do when a prospect says no? Perhaps the best way to handle an objection or an unwillingness to make a commitment is to determine the nature of the problem. Have you determined an appropriate ask level? Is your timing right? Have you arranged for an appropriate environment in which to make the request or are there distractions? Is the objection the result of a simple misunderstanding?

Attempt to get to the root of the objection and address any issues or problems directly and honestly. You may discover that the objection can be easily resolved or that you need follow-up steps. Alternately, you

FIGURE 2-13. SAMPLE PLEDGE LETTER

[Your Nonprofit Name and Address]

Dear [**Your Executive Director's Name**]:

Because of my strong belief in the mission of [**your nonprofit name**], and my desire to make a difference in the lives of [**personalize here**], I hereby pledge [**insert amount**]. I wish for this pledge to be used for the purposes of [**personalize here**].

Enclosed is my initial payment of [**insert amount**] on my pledge of [**insert amount**]. I wish for my pay out schedule to be [**personalize here, for example, monthly, yearly**]. Please send me a reminder when a payment is due.

Please be aware of [**insert any special circumstances such as financial or personal obligations**]. [optional: If I cannot fulfill this pledge because of my death, please consider this pledge an obligation of my estate.]

Thank you for this wonderful opportunity to strengthen [**personalize here**].

Sincerely yours,

[**Prospect's name**]

---

may decide to settle for a gift amount that is less than what you had hoped. It is important to address objections; however, do not lose your focus on the solicitation. Redirect the conversation to the business at hand. In any case, remember that all gifts at all levels are important, that all donors should be valued and respected, and that everything you do lays the groundwork for the next potential gift.

THE IMPORTANCE OF DIVERSIFICATION

To build a strong financial foundation for your nonprofit, you must diversify your funding base. This means seeking government and private funding and cultivating a broad constituency that includes individual, foundation, and corporate supporters. Such diversification is critically important (Seltzer, 1987) and will help to ensure fiscal stability in the midst of an ever-changing philanthropic environment.

In diversifying your funding base, keep in mind that different types of foundations exist. The unique characteristics of private foundations, operating foundations, corporate foundations, and community foundations are discussed in chapter 4. Remember that many corporations have giving programs that operate completely separate from their corporate foundations. Such programs are addressed in more detail in chapter 6.

Although this book is not intended to instruct you in the art of proposal writing, the following list is typical of the information most foundation and corporate proposals require:

- summary statement or paragraph
- need/problem statement
- project description
- goals and objectives
- project activities
- evaluation plan
- agency capability
- organization and project budget
- future and other funding
- cover letter.

Also consider the following when writing funding proposals:

- Use active voice.
- Make it readable and use lay language.
- Be specific about the problem you are addressing.
- Make it concise and to the point.
- Use a single writer.
- Have an in-house and outside person review the proposal before submission.
- *Check and recheck application guidelines.*
- Keep copies of everything submitted.
- Check to make sure your proposal is received on time.

For more detailed information on proposal writing, consult *Getting Funded: A Complete Guide to Proposal Writing* by Hall (1988), *Proposal Writing* by Coley and Scheinberg (1990), "Preparing Effective Proposals" by Brody (1991), *Guide to Proposal Writing* by Geever and McNeill (1993), or *Winning Grants Step by Step* by Carlson (1995).

ACKNOWLEDGMENT AND STEWARDSHIP

Saying "thank you" to donors may seem a less important task than the many other things you must remember when fundraising; however, it is an essential part of your fundraising program. Donors like to feel appreciated.

Your nonprofit should establish clear procedures to thank funders. Thank you notes or letters should be prompt, personal, and thoughtfully written. Gifts at all levels must be acknowledged.

A general rule in thanking donors is to "match" the thank you with the level and type of gift. For example, higher-level gifts may require a more personal response from a key executive or your board president, and lower-level donors may be thanked in a less personal manner by staff or a peer. In any case, remember that each donor is an individual who was prompted to give for a personal reason. The more thoughtful you can be in acknowledging that reason, the more effective your thank you will be. Form letters are clearly the least desirable written response and handwritten notes the best. A telephone call to thank a donor can be wonderful, but a phone call should never take the place of a written acknowledgment. Put yourself in the shoes of the donor and try to imagine a perfect response to the gift. Also keep in mind that thanking is an important form of cultivation; if done thoughtfully, it can create much goodwill and strongly influence future giving.

Donor recognition requires creativity. Often, a major gift or a lead gift in a campaign warrants recognition beyond a thank you letter or phone call. Do not rely on the standard bronze plaque unless you know that this is the ideal method to thank a donor. Recognition can come in many forms. Take flowers to a donor who just chaired a special event, create permanent naming opportunities in your facility to acknowledge giving at certain levels, arrange for a special gathering or event to recognize donor contributions, or publish a donor honor roll in your nonprofit's newsletter.

In some cases, donor recognition may involve a press release or press conference. Attempt in all cases to tailor gift recognition to meet the needs of a particular donor. Do not make assumptions or generalizations about donor recognition. Some donors, particularly those who make very large gifts, may wish to remain anonymous; this should always be an option.

Some organizations use gift clubs that promise special perquisites, such as dinner with the board president; tickets to events; or offerings such as mugs, neckties, or T-shirts. To avoid reporting or deduction requirements instituted by the IRS, your nonprofit must keep the market value of such perks at less than 2 percent of the gift value. Thanking a donor with a gift at any level is not a problem, but when nonprofits use perks as a sort of quid pro quo, it can become a problem. Play it safe, and do not market perks when seeking gifts. Then, when and if you offer a donor something as a thank you, it will truly be that.

Be aware that IRS requires certain wording regarding the use of goods and services for gifts. Chapter 5 includes information about IRS regulations regarding the acknowledgment of gifts.

Your nonprofit should have procedures in place to provide stewardship reports to donors who give to a particular program or activity or give to establish an endowed fund. You should regularly update donors on how their gift support is being used or, in the case of endowment, how well the fund has prospered. An annual financial stewardship report should be sent to the donor providing such information as the book and market value of the fund, the growth over the previous year, and the rate of interest accrued. The report also should inform the donor of the level of this year's payout and the anticipated payout rate for the coming year.

REFERENCES

Brody, R. (1991). Preparing effective proposals. In R. L. Edwards & J. A. Yankey (Eds.), *Skills for effective human services management.* Washington, DC: NASW Press, pp. 44–61.

Carlson, M. (1995). *Winning grants: Step by step.* San Francisco: Jossey-Bass.

Coley, S. M., & Scheinberg, C. A. (1990). *Proposal writing.* Newbury Park, CA: Sage Publications.

Dundjerski, M. (1995, September 7). United Way: 1% increase in gifts. *The Chronicle of Philanthropy, 7*(22), 27–29.

Duronio, M. A. (1993). *Professional in philanthropy: Fund raisers at work.* Unpublished manuscript, University of Pittsburgh, Pittsburgh, PA.

Edwards, R. L., & Austin, D. M. (1991). Managing effectively in an environment of competing values. In R. L. Edwards & J. A. Yankey (Eds.), *Skills for effective human services management.* Washington, DC: NASW Press, pp. 5–26.

Geever, J. C., & McNeill, P. (1993). *Guide to proposal writing.* New York: The Foundation Center.

Hall, M. S. (1988). *Getting funded: A complete guide to proposal writing.* (3rd ed.). Portland, OR: Continuing Education Publications, Portland State University.

Kaplan, A. E. (Ed.). (1996). *Giving USA—1996.* New York: AAFRC Trust for Philanthropy.

Klein, K. (1994). *Fundraising for social change.* (3rd ed.). Inverness, CA: Chardon Press.

Quinn, R. E. (1988). *Beyond rational management: Mastering the paradoxes and competing demands of high performance.* San Francisco: Jossey-Bass.

Read, P. E. (Ed.). (1986). *Foundation fundamentals: A guide for grantseekers.* (3rd ed.) New York: The Foundation Center.

Seltzer, M. (1987). *Securing your organization's future: A complete guide to fundraising strategies.* New York: The Foundation Center.

Seymour, H. J. (1988). *Designs for fund-raising.* Rockville, MD: Fund-Raising Institute/The Taft Group.

Turner, J. B. (1995). Fundraising and philanthropy. In R. L. Edwards (Ed.-in-Chief), *Encyclopedia of social work* (19th ed., Vol. 2, pp. 1038–1044). Washington, DC: NASW Press.

Wood, E. W. (1991). The six key concepts of major gift fund-raising. *The skill and art of major gift fund-raising.* Workshop presented at the University of North Carolina at Chapel Hill, June 3–4, 1991.

Worth, M. J. (1993). *Educational fund raising: Principles and practice.* Phoenix, AZ: Oryx Press.

FUNDAMENTALS OF PLANNED GIVING

by June Steel

W henever a donor makes a gift to a nonprofit, an element of planning exists. The term "planned giving" can be interpreted in
different ways. Sometimes planned giving refers to the type of asset to
give (for example, cash, stock, or land) or the way to make a gift (for
example, current gift, life income gift, or bequest). At other times,
planned giving refers specifically to "deferred gifts." Deferred gifts made
immediately will benefit your nonprofit at some point in the future. In
either case, planned giving enables the gift to work in the best interests
of the donor and the nonprofit.

In this chapter, we consider a broad interpretation of planned giving
while also focusing on deferred gifts. We discuss issues to consider when
establishing a planned giving program and consider some of the "nuts and
bolts" of getting started. Strategies to establish and market planned giving
programs are reviewed, as are planned giving methods that include outright gifts, bequests, gifts of life insurance, and gifts of real and personal
property. Finally, we describe life income gift vehicles including charitable
remainder trusts, pooled income funds, and charitable gift annuities.

THE ADVANTAGES OF PLANNED GIVING

Planned gifts have many advantages, both to the donor and the nonprofit. For many donors, planned gifts provide an opportunity to enjoy

*June Steel is the director of planned gifts, Office of Development, The University of North Carolina
at Chapel Hill.*

the intrinsic value and personal satisfaction that come from giving a larger gift to a nonprofit than they otherwise might be able to afford. The donor may receive recognition for the gift while he or she is still alive. Significant tax advantages also may exist when making a planned gift. Such tax advantages include removal of the asset from the donor's estate, thus reducing the estate tax, avoidance of all or part of the capital gains tax that would be incurred if the gift asset were sold, and a charitable gift income tax deduction. In addition, the donor often is able to give a low-yielding asset to a gift vehicle that produces life income and actually receive more income during his or her life than the asset itself would yield.

The advantages of planned gifts for your nonprofit are numerous. A planned gift is frequently larger than outright gifts. Often, a planned gift is irrevocable, and although your nonprofit may not have use of the gift until some point in the future, the assets become the property of your organization at the time the gift is made. In the case of irrevocable gifts, the value of the gift can be added to your gift record system and counted toward a campaign goal. To learn about rules for determining how such gifts should be counted, consult *Managing Reporting Standards for Educational Institutions: Fund Raising and Related Activities*, published by the Council for Advancement and Support of Education (CASE). Planned gifts also provide an opportunity for your nonprofit to develop a close long-term relationship with a donor. This relationship often leads to additional giving.

THE ROLE OF PLANNED GIVING IN YOUR NONPROFIT

Planned giving to nonprofits has become more complex over the past several years, particularly with regard to the tax consequences of such gifts. Building a strong foundation for your nonprofit requires that you be aware of the various ways that donors can make a gift and the ramifications of each method. In chapter 2, the fundraising process was illustrated as a spiral of prospect identification, information, interest, involvement, and investment. A donor typically may give an annual gift, later increase the level of support to a major gift, and eventually make a very large, or ultimate, gift. Frequently, planned gifts are an important component of both major and ultimate gifts.

Experts predict that trillions of dollars will change hands in the next several years (Panas, 1984). This shift in the control of wealth means enormous potential for gifts to your nonprofit. However, tremendous competition for these gifts will exist. To be successful, you must understand the different types of planned giving strategies, tools, methods, and opportunities.

If your nonprofit does not have the resources to devote a staff person to planned giving activities—and most nonprofits do not have this luxury—your organization's director and other staff members who will be involved in fundraising must have a working knowledge of this specialized area of development. Extraordinary planned giving opportunities will likely develop in the future, but to take full advantage of these opportunities, you must take steps to ensure that your organization is well positioned. These steps include establishing policies and guidelines for receiving planned gifts and developing a marketing program to inform and educate your supporters and the larger community. You also must have access to counsel from lawyers and accountants who have specialized expertise in planned giving. Often this counsel may come from members of your board or other volunteers.

An effective development effort has several components, each of which is important and contributes to your program's overall success. A first step in determining whether your nonprofit should implement a planned giving program is to engage staff and board members in looking at your organization's mission and determining the level of resources needed to carry out that mission now and in the future. Determine what level of support is needed to accomplish fundraising activities to meet your immediate operating needs as well as future needs. Planned gifts should never be viewed as competing with outright gifts. Rather, planned giving programs provide donors with several options for structuring gifts that are in addition to and different from outright giving. Planned giving programs must be integrated into your overall development effort.

Before seeking planned gifts, your nonprofit should have a well-thought-out fundraising program. Analyze your nonprofit, and assess the role that private dollars play in your financial picture. Consider the following questions:

+ Does your organization live from month to month and rely heavily on private donations for general operating expenses?
+ Do you expect that your organization will be a viable entity far into the future, or is it fulfilling a short-term need in the community?

Planned gifts are made in the present, but often their benefits will not be available until some point far into the future. Thus, a planned giving strategy is not the fundraising approach to use if your nonprofit needs current operating dollars or if you are not likely to be in existence over the long term. It takes years to build a planned giving "pipeline," and your nonprofit must have the capacity and willingness to devote resources (money and time) now to reap rewards in the future.

If the results of your organizational analysis indicate that a planned giving program makes sense for your nonprofit, you should begin educating staff and board members about basic planned giving concepts. Such an education can be accomplished through identifying and attending a planned giving conference or workshop as well as asking planned giving professionals in your community for advice and counsel. You may find it useful to identify other nonprofits in your area with a similar mission, size, and budget, and engage in efforts to develop informal networks. In this way, you can seek information about other nonprofits' experiences with planned giving and explore the viability of establishing a planned giving program in your organization.

Once you are comfortable with your decision to move forward with a planned giving program, engage your staff and volunteers in developing a proposal to present to your board. The proposal should address the different types of planned giving instruments, including outright gifts, bequests, life income gifts, charitable lead trusts, revocable charitable trusts, and insurance policies (Figure 3-1). All these instruments are discussed in this chapter. After the board endorses such a

FIGURE 3-1. OVERVIEW OF SOME PLANNED GIVING INSTRUMENTS

Type of Gift	Form of Gift	Benefit to Donor	Benefit to Nonprofit
OUTRIGHT GIFT	• cash • securities • real estate • insurance • personal property	• deductible for income-tax purposes	• funds available for immediate use by organization

BEQUESTS: Anything one owns at the time of death may be passed on to an organization or person through one's last will and testament. Moreover, all forms of life income gifts may be in testamentary form to benefit family or friends and will then become available for use by named organizations.

LIFE INCOME GIFTS

Type of Gift	Form of Gift	Benefit to Donor	Benefit to Nonprofit
A. pooled income funds	• appreciated securities • cash	• variable income that may provide hedge against inflation • tax deduction when gift is made • no capital gains tax on appreciated gift	• ensures future funding
B. charitable remainder unitrusts	• real estate • securities • cash	• same as pooled income fund plus: • can be tailored to donor's situation • permits deferred income • includes real estate	• ensures substantial future funding
C. charitable remainder annuity trusts	• cash • securities	• fixed income • tax deduction in year that gift is made • no capital gains tax on appreciated gift; alternative minimum tax may apply	• ensures substantial future funding
D. charitable gift annuity	• cash • securities	• fixed income for lifetime • tax deduction in early years of gift	• portion of funds can be available to organization • ensures future funding • upon death of insured, remaining principal payable to organization

CHARITABLE LEAD TRUST	• cash • securities • real estate	• allows property to be passed to others with little or no shrinkage due to taxes	• provides organization with current income for the length of the trust for a period of ten years
REVOCABLE CHARITABLE TRUST	• cash • securities • real estate	• all or part of amount placed in trust is available if needed by donor • removes burden of managing assets	• very high percentage of revocable trusts are not revoked and thus provide future funding

INSURANCE POLICIES

A. organization is made owner and beneficiary of policy currently in force	• life insurance	• donor gets income tax deduction for value of policy when transferred • future premium payments may be deducted as gift • donor can make large future gift at small present cost	• organization may borrow on • organization cash in policy • organization may receive face value of policy at insured's death
B. paid-up policy is given to organization	• life insurance	• tax deduction based on current value of policy	• organization may keep policy and receive face value upon death of insured
C. organization is named beneficiary of policy but not owner	• life insurance	• enables donor to make large future gift at small present cost • donor may change beneficiary later • donor may borrow on policy	• upon death of insured, organization will receive face value of policy

Source: KPMG Peat Marwick, *Management Issue*.
Note: This table was revised by the AAFRC Trust for Philanthropy. The trust gratefully acknowledges the advice of the National Committee on Planned Giving. The contents of the table are the responsibility of the trust. This table is for information purposes only and is not a substitute for legal or other professional advice.

Source: Kaplan, A. E. (Ed.). (1996). Giving USA—1996. New York: AAFRC Trust For Philanthropy. Reprinted with permission.

plan in concept, determine clear policies and guidelines that detail how your organization will solicit, close, and manage planned gifts.

THE NUTS AND BOLTS OF A PLANNED GIVING PROGRAM

Many things should be considered when establishing your planned giving program. Foremost among these is the need to establish a comprehensive record-keeping system. Such a system can be kept in both hard copy and a computer file, but attention must be given to the security of the information. Keep planned giving documents and a list or inventory of all the gifts that you expect to receive in a locked file cabinet. Some people will let you know that they have included your nonprofit in their estate plans and will share with you relevant documents; others will tell you of their plans but will not share details. Some individuals will include your organization in their wills and may not let you know. Thus, you may know nothing about a gift until you receive notice of it, usually after the donor has died. You may be surprised to open a letter from an attorney or other estate executor and learn that your nonprofit will be receiving a planned gift.

Create a manual for each type of gift your nonprofit offers. The manual should include a calendar, an outline of procedures, sample letters, enclosures and gift documents, and relevant background information. If you determine in advance how you will handle a gift from the initial inquiry to closure, you will be effective in your planned giving program. At least twice a year, review all your manuals. As you become more experienced, you will discover or develop easier and better procedures and materials.

Once you have created appropriate materials and record-keeping systems, you should identify prospective donors. The profile of a planned giving donor is varied. Older donors to your organization who have substantial assets may be a good place to start. Note that planned giving donors are often difficult to categorize. Many people spend their whole lives accumulating assets and, to the pleasure of many nonprofits, want those assets to make a difference in their communities. Others may have children or other heirs, and they may want to give part of their assets to them and part to the causes they support. Sometimes people you least expect to have substantial assets are good prospects for planned giving because they may have lived frugally or inherited assets. Because planned giving prospects vary, do not make snap judgments or assumptions about an individual's capacity to give. Treat every inquiry with respect, and often a gift will follow.

An effective method of acquiring planned giving donors is through self-identification. Almost always, self-identification comes about as a result of a strong, broad-based marketing program. A marketing program can be simple or comprehensive. However, the goal is to present a clear, consistent message and to repeat that message again and again. Let potential donors know what your nonprofit does, what your financial needs are, what gift methods are available, and whom to call for information about planned giving opportunities. Examples of inexpensive yet effective materials include a simple check-off box on a gift receipt, an advertisement or article in your newsletter, or a small brochure produced on your computer. As you prepare your marketing materials for planned giving, consider your mission, audience, budget, topic, and timing. Do only what you can afford. To be effective, you must be prepared to respond to each inquiry, so be sure you have a plan in place. Draft follow-up letters in advance so you can quickly produce a personalized response to each inquiry. A prompt response shows that you care. A slow response may cause you to lose a wonderful gift opportunity.

In all development work, but particularly in planned giving, you must be worthy of a donor's trust. Donors will often tell you about their hopes and dreams as they explain why and how they want to make a gift. Tell potential donors to take care of themselves first, then consider how they can help your organization. If you care about donors, they will feel your sincerity. Listening is crucial in planned giving activity. Some individuals know exactly what they want to give and how, but many do not. Although planned gifts are structured in tax-advantaged ways, the gift, or the donor's charitable intent, must be the primary focus. Those staff and volunteers involved in soliciting planned gifts must ensure that their actions support this premise. Frequently, a strong bond develops between a donor and the staff member or volunteer involved in the planned giving effort. The National Committee on Planned Giving established the *Model Standards of Practice for the Charitable Gift Planner* (1991) outlining the expectation that all transactions will be handled in an ethical manner. Full disclosure is absolutely essential. You need to share with the donor all relevant information so his or her decision is well-informed.

Finally, when working with a potential planned gift donor, share as much information as possible but never offer advice. Advice should be given only by professionals retained by the donor, such as attorneys, tax consultants, and trust officers.

Sometimes a donor will ask you to consult directly with a legal or financial advisor. This is a wonderful opportunity to talk with the person who knows the donor's financial status in detail and understands the technical aspects of giving methods. This opportunity also may lead to your developing a relationship with the donor's advisor that can be useful in the future, with you truly becoming a team, working with and for the donor. Often, your largest gifts will come out of this type of collaboration.

SOLICITING AND STEWARDING PLANNED GIFTS

In planned giving, a personal visit is usually the best approach to gift solicitation. Planned giving can be technical, and it is helpful to the solicitor to see the donor's face as options are explained. Facial expressions and body language can give valuable clues as to whether a donor is understanding what you are saying. Always approach the conversation in simple terms, and become more specific and technical as the donor's questions require. If possible, take a written proposal and a chart of calculations with you to discuss and leave with the donor. If a personal visit is not an option, phone conversations can help to build necessary rapport and trust.

When a donor makes a gift, he or she is demonstrating a belief in your organization and a trust that the gift will be used in accordance with his or her wishes. Make a special effort to thank each of your donors often and sincerely. As in major gift cultivation, you may consider sending your planned giving donors holiday greetings and birthday cards, as well as copies of your organization's newsletters. Provide your donors with information about how their gifts are being used to help your nonprofit and those you serve. Whenever possible, write personal notes, because such efforts pay off. One day, a previous donor called to indicate that she wanted to make a gift. She had made gifts to other organizations in years past but had decided to make only one gift this time. She had selected us. Why? Because we had sent her cards over the years and had always included a personal note with the quarterly check she received for a life income gift. Knowing that we cared was important to her.

Depending on the value of the gift, you might make a personal visit to the donor or host an event in his or her honor. Another approach is the creation of a planned giving "society" that includes all donors who have made a planned gift, regardless of the level. Membership in such a group tells the donor that you value him or her. Because you may work with donors for many years, you must thank them often. Many of your next gifts will come from satisfied donors. Chapter 2 addresses more fully the many meaningful ways you can thank your donors.

PLANNED GIVING INSTRUMENTS

In planned giving, you should be aware of the types of assets a donor can give to your nonprofit and alert to the issues associated with each. Different types of planned giving instruments or vehicles exist; the most common of these are identified in Figure 3-1. The following instruments will be described in terms of benefits to both the recipient organization and the donor.

Outright Gifts

Your nonprofit can use an outright gift immediately. As shown in Figure 3-1, outright gifts include cash, securities, real estate, insurance, or personal property. The value of such a gift is deductible for income tax purposes in accordance with IRS policy.

Cash

Cash is the most popular type of charitable outright gift and usually comes in the form of a personal check. The gift date, for the donor's tax purposes, is the day that the check is hand-delivered or postmarked by the U.S. Postal Service. A donor also can contribute using a credit card. In this case, the gift date is the day the gift is charged, even though the account will likely be paid later. Gifts of cash also may be conveyed through bank drafts, which are instructions from a donor to his or her bank directing that money be periodically transferred to your nonprofit. Gifts of cash are fully deductible up to 50 percent of the donor's adjusted gross income. If all the deduction cannot be taken in the year of the gift, the deduction can be carried forward for up to five additional years. This is an important provision for retired people who may have a low taxable income.

Securities

If a donor gives securities, such as stocks or bonds, to your nonprofit he or she receives a federal income tax deduction equal to the fair market value of the securities at the time of the gift. A donor typically fares far better if he or she gives your organization the asset, not the cash received after sale of the asset. For example, if the securities are sold by the donor and the cash from the sale is then donated to your nonprofit, the donor is required to pay capital gains tax on any appreciated value. However, if the donor gives your nonprofit the securities and you then sell them, the capital gains tax is avoided. Gifts of appreciated assets are fully deductible up to 30 percent of the donor's adjusted gross income for that year. Any excess over the 30 percent deduction can be carried forward for up to five additional years.

Donors can hold stock two ways—in certificate form or in a brokerage account. If the stock is held in certificate form, the donor can make a gift by delivering the certificates directly to your organization. The certificate should not be endorsed, but it should be accompanied by a stock power. To ensure safe delivery, the certificate and stock power should be mailed in separate envelopes. The stock power should include only the signature of the donor and that signature should be guaranteed by a bank officer. The bank officer should not date the signature guarantee.

If the stock is held in a brokerage account, the donor can instruct the bank or broker to deliver the securities to you by electronic transfer. When your nonprofit anticipates receiving gifts of securities, it may be wise to open an account with a brokerage firm that can accept delivery and handle the sale of such gifts.

The gift date for securities is the date that they pass unconditionally from the donor's control. For most securities, the value of the gift is the market value of the stock. Market values are determined by calculating the mean between the high and the low quotations on the gift date, which can be obtained from the financial pages of newspapers the day following the gift or obtained electronically on the same day after the stock market closes.

Real Property

Gifts of real property can be a personal or vacation home, a farm or ranch, a commercial building, or an undeveloped piece of land. The gift can be the entire property or part of the property. A donor can make an outright property gift or in some cases transfer the property to a gift vehicle that generates life income. Such life income gifts are discussed later in this chapter. A donor also may transfer property to your nonprofit, while retaining the right to live in or on it. When the donor dies, your organization can then sell or use the property. This type of transaction is complicated and should be considered only under certain circumstances. An example of when this type of transaction may be worth exploring is if a donor lives adjacent to your building and he or she offers this arrangement. Otherwise, in many cases the potential problems outweigh the benefits.

With gifts of real property, potential environmental issues can be a major concern. Before your organization accepts any property gift, be certain that the property is free from environmental hazards. If you accept ownership of contaminated land, cleanup may become your responsibility. Needless to say, this can be extraordinarily costly. You should have an environmental impact study done before accepting any property gift. Seek input from a local real estate professional who can advise you on what level of impact study you should have done and refer you to companies in your area that do such studies.

Life Insurance

A gift of life insurance can be made to your nonprofit in two ways. One option is to make your nonprofit the *beneficiary* of a new or existing policy; the other option is to make your nonprofit the *owner* of a new or existing policy. If a donor owns a policy and wishes to make your organization the beneficiary, a substantial gift may be in store for you. However, the owner has the right to change the beneficiary at any time, and no charitable deduction exists for the donor. Positive estate tax implications exist with this type of arrangement and can be explained by a tax consultant. If a donor makes your nonprofit the owner of a new or existing policy, you have available an immediate charitable deduction that is approximately equal to the cash value of the policy. The donor will continue to pay any remaining premiums, which also are tax deductible.

Insurance is an easy gift to receive and hold until policy maturity. As long as the donor continues to pay required premiums, your nonprofit simply lists the policy as an asset and continues to keep in close touch with the donor. Many people have policies that they no longer need; they were purchased while children were young and resources limited. Now, with the original need for the insurance no longer a factor, some individuals are happy to give these policies to you. Keep a listing of them in your planned giving inventory.

Your nonprofit must be cautious about receiving gifts of life insurance. To show the financial benefits of insurance, agents sometimes present to potential buyers unrealistic premium projections. Many projections are overly optimistic, and unexpected additional premium payments are required. This situation can be embarrassing for the donor and can lead to a policy lapsing. To avoid this scenario, review closely the terms of the policies and the payment schedules with your donors; when possible, seek expert advice from a volunteer or board member.

Personal Property

Personal property that can be donated to a nonprofit includes such items as rare books, manuscripts, paintings, artifacts, and other art objects. Your organization should first determine whether the item supports the mission of the organization. For example, a theater group can accept vintage clothing for use in its performances. In this case, a direct relationship exists between the item and the nonprofit. If you can demonstrate such a relationship, the donor is entitled to a charitable deduction equal to the full fair market value of the donated item. If your organization cannot use the gift, you may still accept it, but the donor's charitable deduction is limited to the initial cost of the object rather than its fair market value. In either case, the charitable deduction is limited to 30 percent of the donor's adjusted gross income and can be carried forward for up to five additional years.

Special Rules Related to Outright Gifts

All gifts other than cash require special handling. The IRS requires that all charitable organizations maintain detailed records of all gifts of property, other than publicly traded stocks and bonds, with a value greater than $500. Nonprofits must maintain records on the location of donated property, how the property is related to the nonprofit's tax-exempt purpose, and if sold, how it was sold and the sale price. Nonprofits also should be familiar with IRS forms 8283 and 8282, which pertain to appraisal and substantiation rules. Lack of compliance can be costly. For instance, if your nonprofit sells property it received as a gift within two years of receipt, the nonprofit must file form 8282 within a prescribed period or the organization will be liable for a daily penalty.

Deferred Gifts

Bequests

Many people are surprised to learn that millions of Americans die each year without a will. When these people die, state law determines the disposition of their assets. Consequently, wealth that could be directed to nonprofits is lost.

Your nonprofit should encourage supporters to make a will or bequest and include in their will a gift to your nonprofit. When a donor makes such a gift, the gift is fully deductible for estate tax purposes. Many nonprofits find that starting a planned giving program with will or bequest gifts is relatively simple and inexpensive. Although an individual can change his or her will at any time and your nonprofit may be dropped as a beneficiary, you have nothing to lose by making prospects and donors aware of this giving option.

Three types of bequest gifts exist: specific, residuary, and contingent bequest gifts. A specific bequest indicates that a specific amount will be given to a charitable organization. This bequest may be cash, securities, or real or tangible personal property. A residuary bequest names your nonprofit to receive all, or a percentage, of the remainder of the estate after specific bequests have been fulfilled. A contingent bequest shows a gift to your nonprofit but takes effect only if all other beneficiaries named in the will have died. If your nonprofit is named a contingent beneficiary, proceeds will come to you, rather than the state, when there are no remaining living beneficiaries.

Life Income Gifts

On a continuum between outright gifts and bequest gifts, life income gifts are in the middle. With a life income gift, an asset is irrevocably given to your nonprofit. The asset is then invested, and some or all of the income earnings are paid to a designated beneficiary or beneficiaries. In most cases, the donor or family members are the beneficiaries. Your organization can use the gift or asset when the beneficiary dies.

Most planned giving programs offer three kinds of life income arrangements: charitable remainder trusts, pooled income funds, and charitable gift annuities.

Because a donor or designated beneficiary receives income over the course of his or her lifetime, life income gifts offer limited charitable tax benefits, and a donor may receive a charitable deduction for only a portion of the value of the assets given. On a positive note, when a donor gives appreciated assets to a charitable remainder trust or to a pooled income fund, all capital gains tax is avoided. Gifts to a charitable gift annuity avoid part of the capital gains tax.

Charitable Remainder Trusts

A charitable remainder trust is similar to other types of trusts except that it has a charitable beneficiary. A donor transfers an asset irrevocably to a trust and specifies how the income and principal are to be distributed. The trust can be established during life or at death, and it can be for the life of the beneficiary or for a term of up to 20 years.

Two types of charitable remainder trusts exist: a unitrust and an annuity trust. A unitrust pays a variable income based on a percentage of the fair market value of the trust's assets. The assets are revalued annually. An annuity trust pays a fixed income each year, which is at least 5 percent of the market value of the assets at the time the trust is established.

A trust program is not required for your nonprofit to receive trust gifts. A trust is simply a legal document drafted by an attorney and managed and invested, usually by a financial institution. Often, a nonprofit does not know that charitable trusts have been set up and may learn of the gift only when the proceeds are received.

Pooled Income Fund

A pooled income fund is similar to a mutual fund—donor contributions are "pooled" for investment purposes. The net income of a pooled fund is distributed to the donors on the basis of the number and value of "shares" held by each.

Gifts to a pooled income fund are irrevocable, and donors receive an income tax charitable deduction based on the age of the beneficiary(ies) and the performance of the fund. Income payments to the beneficiary(ies) are taxed as ordinary income. A donor can name two beneficiaries to receive an income for life, but each must be at least 50 years old when designated.

Charitable Gift Annuity

A charitable gift annuity is a life income vehicle that pays a donor a fixed dollar amount for life, in exchange for an irrevocable gift to your nonprofit. The donor receives an income tax deduction for the nonannuity portion of the gift. Furthermore, a portion of the income received each year by the donor is tax free. However, regulations for gift annuities vary from state to state, so check your state's regulations.

A deferred charitable gift annuity is a variation that allows a donor to defer the income until a later date, such as when he or she retires. Because the assets are allowed to grow for many years, the rate of return that the donor receives is typically higher than with a current gift annuity. The rate is still applied against the original amount of the gift and not the appreciated value; however, the delayed payout often enables the donor to claim a large percentage of the gift value as a charitable deduction.

For your nonprofit to offer a pooled income fund or charitable gift annuities as a giving option, you must establish specific programs. These steps require a commitment from your board of directors, allocation of some additional resources, and a critical mass of potential donors. Both programs can be managed by the nonprofit, but most nonprofits look to outside sources for expertise and assistance. These programs are complicated, require fastidious attention to detail for many years, and should probably not be considered until your fundraising program is well established.

CONCLUSION

Planned giving programs can offer extraordinary opportunities for your nonprofit. Analyze carefully the needs of your organization, research the potential for such a program, and develop a realistic plan. Then implement more prudently but enthusiastically.

REFERENCES

Kaplan, A. E. (Ed.). (1996). *Giving USA—1996.* New York: AAFRC Trust for Philanthropy.

National Committee on Planned Giving. (1991). *Model standards of practice for the charitable gift planner.* Indianapolis: Author.

Panas, J. (1984). *Megagifts: Who gives them, who gets them.* Chicago: Pluribus Press.

CHAPTER 4

BASICS OF PROSPECT RESEARCH

Prospect research is the investigative process through which an organization that wants to raise funds identifies prospective donors of grants or philanthropic gifts, assesses their gift capacity and potential, and uncovers facts that may show how an optimum size gift may best be solicited. (Jenkins & Lucas, 1985, p. 2)

Research is the foundation of all successful fundraising. Good prospect research ensures that you will be effective and efficient in your major gift activities. Research enables you to identify and focus your efforts to cultivate individuals, foundations, and corporations that have the capacity to give and interest in your organization. Research helps you avoid wasted efforts on prospects who have limited capacity to make significant gifts or who have shown that their philanthropic interests lie elsewhere. Once you have identified individuals or organizations with gift capacity and likely intent, you have taken an important step in securing significant support.

This chapter addresses the process of researching individual, corporate, and foundation prospects. We also provide information about electronic and print resources to aid in your prospect research efforts.

THE PROCESS OF RESEARCHING INDIVIDUAL PROSPECTS

Individual prospect research is a process that involves three basic steps: identifying prospects, researching or gathering information about them, and rating them.

Identifying Individual Prospects

An excellent place to start to identify prospects is an examination of your current list of supporters, including current and past donors, board and committee members, volunteers, and others who are involved with your nonprofit. Such an examination will likely lead you to conclude that there are many current donors who have been giving at a nominal level but are capable of giving much larger gifts. These same individuals may help you identify others who have not been giving but have the capacity.

Members of your organization's board of trustees are often excellent major gift prospects. Ideally, your board membership will be balanced in terms of members' wealth, wisdom, and willingness to work. Of course, not all your members will have all three of these characteristics; indeed, you will be lucky if many possess at least two. Nevertheless, although not all your board members should be appointed based on their financial capacity, those who have the means to make significant gifts should not be overlooked. Regardless of their personal capacity to give, your board members can help identify individuals in the community who have both the capacity and the possible motivation to make contributions.

In some cases, it may be appropriate to consider as potential prospects those individuals who use your nonprofit's services. This strategy may be good for certain types of nonprofits, such as those involved with the arts, but less viable for some human services organizations that must be concerned about issues of client confidentiality.

Other resources for identifying potential donors are local, regional, or statewide newspapers. Looking through the community and business sections of newspapers can help you identify "movers and shakers." These people have social standing, may have the financial capacity to be major contributors to your organization, or may be willing to help you identify others who do.

Your own ability to network for names is one of the best means of identifying prospective major donors. Of course, simply identifying names of those with financial means is a long way from securing gifts. The process is made easier if the major gift prospects whom you identify have an established interest in the mission of your organization.

Researching Individual Prospects

Once you have identified a potential donor, your next challenge is to gather as much relevant information as you can about this person. Begin by creating a file on the prospect. This file should include a prospect biographical form, as illustrated in chapter 2 in Figure 2-4. This form should include the following information:

+ name
+ home address
+ business title and address
+ business affiliation (including directorships of companies)
+ nonprofit organization and foundation board memberships
+ name of university or preparatory school attended
+ civic and country club affiliations
+ family information (names of spouse, children, and other close relatives)
+ known wealth indicators
+ known philanthropic giving.

If you do not have all the information for the prospect biographical form, research at your local public or university library may enable you to fill in the blanks.

Begin your prospect research with the following sources of information:

+ in-house records
+ reference books
+ electronic databases and online services
+ newspapers and magazines
+ donor interviews and personal contacts.

Start your search by looking through library archives for profiles in the local newspapers or regional business journals. Newspapers often profile prominent local citizens, and regional business journals usually profile an industry leader in each edition. A newspaper or journal profile will provide you with most of the information you need for an initial contact with a prospect. Typically, published profiles include information about the individual's educational and employment history, family, civic involvement, and other interesting personal details. Such information may help you determine the best strategy for making a meaningful contact with the prospect.

The profile also may include a list of nonprofit organizations with which your prospect is affiliated. This information can be helpful as you consider whether the individual is someone you want to try to cultivate and solicit. For instance, if someone on your prospect list is heavily involved with conservative organizations, you may safely assume that the prospect will not donate to liberal causes and vice versa. If you learn that the individual is or has been involved with organizations similar to yours, you should give this prospect additional consideration.

If no published profile of the individual is available, your next step in constructing the initial biographical sketch is to check the reference section of the library for publications such as the Marquis *Who's Who in America* series or other similar biographical indexes. (To obtain information about the *Who's Who* series, contact Marquis *Who's Who*, 121 Chanlon Road, New Providence, NJ 07974.) Entries in biographical resources such as the *Who's Who* series typically include family information, an employment history, and club and organization affiliations. Although these profiles may not provide all the answers needed to construct a complete prospect profile, they will provide useful information as you continue your research.

Once you have obtained this initial biographical information, consider how your prospect's employment may affect his or her giving capacity. Knowing the prospect's place of employment and job title will help you estimate his or her compensation.

If your prospect is a senior officer or the executive director of a publicly held company, the first place to look for compensation information is the company's proxy statement. A proxy statement is a financial disclosure form that must be filed with the Securities and Exchange Commission (SEC) every year, making it a public document. If a copy is not in your local library, you can mail a postcard requesting a copy of the proxy statement to the company's corporate headquarters. This information also is available from the SEC through the World Wide Web (http://www.sec.gov).

The proxy statement may include the prospect's exact salary, bonuses, and other compensation. However, because the federal government requires that such information be provided on only the top five officers, senior officers are often the only employees listed in the proxy. Generally, the chief executive officer, president, senior or executive vice presidents, and sometimes the chief financial officer or chief legal counsel are listed. If the proxy does not list your prospect, look at the salaries of others with a similar job title. Although this approach will not enable you to determine the exact salary of your prospect, you will get a fair estimate of compensation. For example, if your prospect is the senior vice president of sales and the proxy states that the senior vice president of manufacturing earned $300,000 in salary and bonuses, you can safely assume that your prospect does not earn more (or he or she would have been listed) but probably does not earn significantly less.

Another important section of the proxy is the listing of the company's board of directors. If the directors are not employees of the company, they usually receive an annual fee or per diem for time spent in board activities. The amount of this compensation is wide-ranging but often exceeds $10,000 per year and frequently includes annual stock purchase options. This annual fee or per diem may be an excellent source of charitable funds.

The proxy statement also lists an employee's stock ownership in the company. This information is especially important to your fundraising efforts. Often, a gift of appreciated stock is easier to secure than a gift of outright cash. In addition, gifts of appreciated stocks often are larger than cash gifts.

Appreciated stocks have a market value that is higher than the shareholder's original purchase price. As indicated in chapter 3, if appreciated stock is sold, the shareholder must pay a capital gains tax on the profit realized from the sale. However, if the stock is donated to a nonprofit organization with 501(c)(3) tax status, the donor can take a tax deduction for the current value of the stock and does not have to pay capital gains tax. Thus, a gift of appreciated stock to a charitable organization can help the prospective donor significantly reduce his or her tax liability while providing the nonprofit with a larger gift.

Stock ownership acquired through an employer's "option plan" also presents an attractive giving possibility. Although stock option plans vary, companies will generally offer a fixed number of shares at a price less than the market value for a set period. For example, Company ABC offers its employees or directors the option to purchase 1,000 shares of company stock at $10.00 per share. The stock is currently trading on the open market at $20.00. If an employee exercises this option and then sells the stock, he or she will be required to pay capital gains tax on the profit from the sale. However, if an employee makes a charitable gift with some or all of the stock, he or she can reduce or eliminate the capital gains tax burden and increase significantly his or her giving capacity. In this example, if a donor took advantage of the stock option, purchased all 1,000 shares of the stock, and donated it to your organization, the donor could in effect turn a $10,000 gift into a $20,000 gift. A gift such as this would be of great benefit to your nonprofit and the donor would receive a $20,000 charitable deduction.

An important consideration in stock ownership is that it can take on different forms that affect giving. Stock that is directly owned is easily converted to cash by selling it on the open market or by transferring it to another person or organization. Stock that is indirectly owned is often held in the name of a trust, retirement plan, foundation, or family member. These shares cannot be sold or transferred without the approval of another person, if at all. Stock that is held beneficially by a person is owned by someone else. In this case, an individual typically has some influence, such as voting rights, over the stock. The owner of beneficially held stocks is typically an individual's spouse.

If your prospect works for a private company or organization and a proxy statement is not available, there are several books that compile salary statistics by job title and career field. One such resource is *The American Almanac of Jobs and Salaries* (Wright, 1996), which lists average salaries for a large number of job fields. To use this book, you must know your prospect's general job title or description and employment field (for example, corporate management, stockbroker, attorney, or physician). Remember that the salaries listed in the book are estimates. Individuals with similar job titles in similar industries can have vastly different salaries. Nevertheless, an educated estimate of a prospect's salary can be a good starting point in helping you determine giving capacity. Business publications such as *Forbes, SmartMoney,* and *Business Week* also provide salary information. These publications often print the salaries of top industry officials, as well as industry-wide estimates.

Several excellent reference books are available to provide you with additional prospect information. If you know that your prospect is a senior officer at a certain company but are unsure of his or her exact job title, books such as Dun and Bradstreet's *Million Dollar Directory* (1996) or *Standard and Poor's Registry* (McGraw-Hill, 1996) can help. A listing in one of these books typically includes a company's address and phone number, industry in which the company is involved, sales information, number of employees, and information about subsidiaries or the parent company. Both of these resources list many privately and publicly held companies in the United States. *Standard and Poor's Registry* (McGraw-Hill, 1996) includes indexes that cross-reference companies with company officers and directors. These indexes may help you determine your prospect's other board affiliations.

Real estate holdings are another form of wealth that must be considered in researching prospects. A donor who gives annually may be a major gift prospect for your nonprofit if he or she owns land or other real estate that has greatly appreciated. As discussed in chapter 3, a gift of appreciated property to a charitable organization not only offsets the capital gains tax but often enables the donor to make a much larger gift than if he or she were giving cash.

Note that prospect research is not an exact science. Often, the best you can hope for is general information with estimates based on a few facts. In prospect research, you must do the best you can with whatever information is available.

Rating Individual Prospects

Once you have completed a biographical history on your prospect, your next task is to determine his or her giving potential. On average, major gifts typically constitute between 0.5 percent and 2.0 percent of a donor's net worth. The following formulas can be used to determine a prospect's estimated net worth (ENW) and a range of his or her giving capacity:

Salary or estimated salary $\times$ 10 = ENW
Total value of stock ÷ .385 = ENW
Total market value of property ÷ .246 = ENW
Value of company (where person is sole owner) $\times$ 2 = ENW
To determine the prospect's estimated giving capability,
 multiply ENW by .005 and by .02.

By using the formula above, you can get a ballpark estimate of your prospect's net worth and giving potential. However, the formula does not take into account other financial responsibilities that an individual may have, including caring for dependents, college tuition for children, health care issues and costs, and other philanthropic commitments. The amount you seek from a prospect can be determined only after you have tested the validity of the above estimate with the information you have gained through effective cultivation and from others who know the prospect.

You can move from a ballpark giving estimate to a more refined rating of your prospect in several ways. One of the best approaches is to convene a group of board members and volunteers to validate your estimates and provide additional prospect information. Known as "screening" sessions, these gatherings can give you information about things such as children attending private schools, obligations to care for an elderly relative, or a recent business setback. Ask participants to review a list of peers confidentially and give you their best estimate about each prospect's giving capacity. Ask participants to focus only on giving capacity, not intent. Provide a giving range that can be assigned to each prospect. Information gathered from such a process will help you to revise your giving estimates. Essentially, what you are seeking when you involve others in such a process is a validation of your giving capacity estimates.

Researching Corporations and Foundations

In the United States, giving from individuals makes up approximately 88 percent of the total amount of philanthropic dollars given to nonprofits each year (Kaplan, 1996). Corporate and foundation giving accounts for the remainder. The total amount of dollars corporations and foundations provide each year to nonprofits is substantial; therefore, they should not be overlooked as important prospects. However, with corporate and foundation prospects you must do your homework. Nonprofits often waste time and resources on unlikely prospects.

Corporate Research

Although individuals give to nonprofits for a variety of reasons, for-profit corporations or companies typically give with a goal in mind. This goal often is to advance a particular objective, such as increasing business, or being seen as a good corporate citizen. Many corporations are involved in charitable giving both through the corporation itself and through their own corporate foundation. Giving from these two sources may not have similar purposes. Increasingly, corporations also are supporting nonprofits through *cause-related marketing*, a new avenue of philanthropic activity that is discussed in chapter 6. Corporations are run by a collection of people. Thus, a company's charitable giving will often reflect the priorities and values of individuals in powerful positions.

To start your quest for corporate support, remember the fundraising adage, "The closer you are to the corporation, the closer you are to the gift." Start your research by focusing on local corporations. You will probably discover that decision makers in local companies will be many of the same people that you researched as individual prospects.

The first step in corporate research is to place the companies in one of three categories: (1) companies with whom your nonprofit has an established relationship, (2) companies that you know have a history of making charitable donations to similar causes but with whom you do not yet have an established relationship, and (3) local companies who look like good neighbors and clearly warrant further investigation.

Building a Strong Foundation: Fundraising for Nonprofits

To determine whether a corporation falls into the first category, ask the following questions:

- Has the company made any contributions to your nonprofit?
- Does the company or do its employees use your services?
- Do your staff members or volunteers have a personal connection with the company or its executives or directors?

Companies in the first two categories will more likely become viable prospects; therefore, focus your efforts on them before proceeding with the third group.

In a process similar to the one you used for creating biographical files for individual prospects, begin by gathering basic information starting with the company's complete name and mailing address. This information can be found in one of several reference books including the *Million Dollar Directory* (Dun & Bradstreet, 1996) and *Standard and Poor's Registry* (McGraw-Hill, 1996). These reference books will help you determine the nature of the company's business and obtain a listing of its officers and directors.

Once you have obtained this rudimentary information, you will then want to get a sense of the company's fiscal situation. If the company is public, you can acquire financial information from the company's annual report or proxy statement. The annual report is important because it typically offers information about civic involvement as well as a general overview of the company's fiscal health. If the company is privately held, the only financial information that you may uncover is what is contained in the above-mentioned reference books. These books will usually list a company's annual revenues or sales. Although sales figures are not a direct reflection of a company's profitability, they do provide some clues. Another source of information on private companies is profiles in local newspapers or regional business journals.

Determine who in the corporation makes the giving decisions. In smaller companies, it may be the president or owner. In larger companies with well-established giving programs, a particular person may be assigned to review funding requests and make preliminary funding decisions. In this case, proposals are typically forwarded to a committee that makes the final decision.

Gifts-in-kind represent another important aspect of corporate philanthropy. Gifts-in-kind are donations by a company either of its services or products. For example, rather than making a cash gift to a nonprofit, an office supply company may donate copy paper or office furniture. A computer company may donate computer hardware or software and the training to use the products.

Corporate research involves gathering as much information as you can to gain a general picture of a company and its philanthropic interests. Such research will not provide you with all the answers, but it often will provide you with enough information to formulate effective cultivation strategies.

Foundation Research

The first thing you need to know about a foundation is its type. As illustrated in Table 4-1, four types of foundations exist, each with unique characteristics: independent, company-sponsored, operating, and community. As shown in Table 4-1, the type of foundation indicates whether it is likely to be a prospect for your organization or cause.

A first step in foundation research is to examine your nonprofit's mission and financial needs and determine whether these "match" the giving interests and capacity of foundation prospects. Foundations often have specific giving interests or limitations such as highly specific programmatic concerns, limited giving to a particular geographic region, limited types of support (for example, operating, project, or bricks and mortar), and limitations on size of grants.

In your search to identify promising foundation prospects, you will need to collect the following information:

- the foundation's full name, address, telephone and fax numbers, and e-mail address
- the name of the contact person
- giving interests
- past giving (how much and to whom)
- application guidelines
- financial information (asset and giving levels)

- names of key staff, officers, and trustees
- the foundation's history.

The contact person is the individual to whom you should address your correspondence. In large foundations, this person is usually a program officer; in smaller foundations usually the executive director, a staff member, or a designated trustee serves as the contact. You must adhere to a foundation's guidelines regarding inquiries and proposal submissions. Program officers, particularly in large foundations, are typically knowledgeable and influential and can be helpful to you in the application process. Treat program officers and foundation staff as you would individual prospects, carefully and thoughtfully engaging them in a cultivation process.

Determine and adhere to a foundation's grant application requirements. Some foundations require that your funding proposal or grant application be submitted on their application form. They may require strict adherence to length limitations and content. Others will accept a proposal in letter form. Most foundations have strict deadlines for submitting proposals. Note whether the foundation considers the submission date to be the postmark date or the date the proposal is received. Submission deadlines are often set in accordance with trustee meetings when funding decisions are made. Be sure to follow the guidelines! For example, if a foundation wishes to be contacted only by mail, do not phone them. Chapter 2 offers some tips for successful proposal writing.

Obtaining a listing of the officers and trustees of a foundation will help you to determine whether these individuals may support your efforts. You may discover that a personal connection can be made or relationship exists with one of your staff members or volunteers. A personal connection will not ensure that your nonprofit will be funded, but such contacts or relationships can be helpful in matching your needs with the interests of the foundation. Foundations receive many more worthy grant requests than they can fund. A personal connection may help make your request stand out. Finally, knowledge of the foundation's history, such as by whom, when, where, and why it was created, will assist you in understanding its philanthropic focus.

TABLE 4-1. GENERAL CHARACTERISTICS OF FOUR TYPES OF FOUNDATIONS

Foundation Type	Description	Source of Funds	Decision-Making Activity	Grantmaking Requirements	Reporting
Independent Foundation	An independent grant-making organization established to aid social, educational, religious, or other charitable activities.	Endowment generally derived from a single source such as an individual, a family, or a group of individuals. Contributions to endowment limited as to tax deductibility.	Decisions may be made by donor or members of the donor's family; by an independent board of directors or trustees; or by a bank or trust officer acting on the donor's behalf.	Broad discretionary giving allowed but may have specific guidelines and give only in a few specific fields. About 70 percent limit their giving to local area.	Annual information returns (990-PF) filed with IRS must be made available to public. A small percentage issue separately printed annual reports.
Company-Sponsored Foundation	Legally an independent grantmaking organization with close ties to the corporation providing funds.	Endowment and annual contributions from a profit-making corporation. May maintain small endowment and pay out most of contributions received annually in grants, or may maintain endowment to cover contributions in years when corporate profits are down.	Decisions made by board of directors often composed of corporate officials, but which may include individuals with nocorporate affiliation. Decisions may also be made by local company officials.	Giving tends to be in fields related to corporate activities or in communities where corporation operates. Usually give more grants but in smaller dollar amounts than independent foundations.	Same as above.

Operating Foundation	An organization that uses its resources to conduct research or provide a direct service.	Endowment usually provided from a single source, but eligible for maximum deductible contributions from public.	Decisions generally made by independent board of directors.	Makes few, if any, grants. Grants generally related directly to the foundation's program.	Same as above.
Community Foundation	A publicly sponsored organization that makes grants for social, educational, religoius, or other charitable purposes in a specific community or region.	Contributions received from many donors. Usually eligible for maximum tax-deductible contributions from public.	Decisions made by board of directors representing the diversity of the community.	Grants generally limited to charitable organizations in local community.	IRS 990 return available to public. Many publish full guidelines or annual reports.

SOURCE: Feczko, M. M. (Ed.). (1996). The foundation directory—1996 edition. Copyright © 1996 by The Foundation Center, 79 Fifth Avenue, New York, NY 10003. Reprinted with permission.

Several reference books on foundations are available. Begin your foundation research by referring to *The Foundation Directory* (Feczko, 1996). This book is an excellent resource for information on national foundations. You also may seek information from statewide publications. For example, if you work in North Carolina, one such publication is *North Carolina Giving* (Shirley, 1996). Similar publications are available in many other states. Federal law requires all registered foundations to file a Form 990 tax return with the IRS. This form includes a list of the trustees, the foundation's assets, and the amount and recipient of every grant made. A copy of the tax return often can be obtained directly from the foundation.

Nonprofits with little experience in foundation fundraising should start with local or statewide foundations. Successful fundraising with national foundations often takes months or years of planning and cultivation. In addition, when seeking support from a national foundation, demonstrating that you have been successful in securing gifts at the local or state level is often helpful.

ADDITIONAL REFERENCE MATERIALS

Electronic Resources

In the current competitive environment for charitable dollars, computer access to the Internet is a must. A wealth of information is available on the Internet to aid you in your research. The Internet has two distinct but connected areas: the text-based Internet and the graphics-based World Wide Web (Web). Using commercial connections such as Prodigy, CompuServe, or America Online or by establishing an individual connection through an Internet service provider (ISP), you can gain access to the Internet.

Every day, more companies, foundations, and nonprofits are creating home pages on the World Wide Web. Home pages are specially designated areas of the Web where people or organizations can make available whatever information they wish. Many corporations and foundations have filled their home pages with important information.

Foundations, for example, are increasingly putting information about their giving priorities and application requirements on the Web.

As use of the Internet and the Web grows, your prospect research efforts are likely to be greatly aided. For example, to obtain important information about companies, you will no longer have to rely on obtaining their annual reports. Recently, the SEC mandated that all publicly traded companies file such reports electronically (Heller, 1996). If you have access to the Internet, these reports are available free from the SEC's Edgar Web site (http://www.sec.gov). To obtain access to information about a particular company, simply log on to Edgar, click on "Search the Edgar Archives," and then enter the company name. You will get a listing of all the documents on file related to that company.

Some documents may be of particular interest. Form 10-K is a detailed version of the company's annual report and generally will give you information about what the company does, the basics of its industry, its competition, and fiscal status. Schedules 13D and 13G will give you information about stock transactions by key company officials and include the names, affiliations, and amounts of stock of individuals who hold more than 5 percent of the voting stock in the company. Usually, the phone numbers of these individuals also will be listed. Schedule 14A, commonly called the proxy statement, includes information about executive compensation as well as background information on key officers and directors. The proxy statement may give you a glimpse of other holdings that these individuals have or will identify key family relationships.

Another valuable resource is information that is increasingly becoming available in CD-ROM format. One prime example is *FC Search: The Foundation Center's Database on CD-ROM* (The Foundation Center, 1996). Included on this CD is information about more than 40,000 U.S. foundations with descriptions of more than 100,000 grants. Information on more than 150,000 individuals who are foundation trustees, officers, and donors also is available. The CD allows you to select from and combine a total of 19 criteria to develop customized prospect lists. Among the criteria are the grantmaker's name, city, state, type, and geographic focus; establishment date; fields of interest; types of support; total assets; and total giving. Criteria also include information about recipients, including name, city, state, grant amount, and year the grant was received.

Print Resources

Many nonprofits will not have the resources to purchase copies of resource books that are useful in prospect research. However, access to many valuable resources often is easy to obtain. Public and university libraries typically have many of the basic resources you need. In addition, a number of states now have centers that have been established to support nonprofits, and these typically have extensive reference collections that are available. Many foundations also provide resource libraries or centers to help local nonprofits.

Finally, The Foundation Center, based in New York City, has extensive library collections in New York and in Washington, DC, as well as field offices in San Francisco, Cleveland, and Atlanta. For more information about The Foundation Center, you may want to visit its World Wide Web home page (http://fdncenter.org). Appendix B lists the addresses of The Foundation Center offices.

Before purchasing materials to help in your prospect research, you should review various reference materials, such as those discussed above, and create a card catalog. Make notes of those you find most useful, where they are located, and what they contain. As a starting point, we suggest that you examine the *Who's Who* series by Marquis and the following publications of The Foundation Center:
  * *The Foundation Directory, Directory Part 2,* and *Supplement*
  * *Guide to U.S. Foundations, the Trustees, Officers, and Donors*
  * *National Directory of Corporate Giving*
  * *Corporate Foundation Profiles*
  * *The Foundation 1000* (provides in-depth information on the 1,000 largest U.S. foundations)
  * *National Guide to Funding in Arts and Culture*
  * *Guide to Funding for International and Foreign Programs.*

In addition, The Foundation Center publishes several regional directories of foundations or grantmakers as well as a series of grant guides that enable you to focus on foundations that have awarded grants in a specific field of interest. Guides are available for the following fields:

- aging
- alcohol and drug abuse
- arts, culture, and the humanities
- children and youth
- community development, housing, and employment
- crime, law enforcement, and abuse prevention
- elementary and secondary education
- environment protection and animal welfare
- film media and communications
- foreign and international programs
- health programs for children and youth
- higher education
- homelessness
- hospitals, medical care, and research
- libraries and information services
- matching and challenge support
- minorities
- people with physical and mental disabilities
- public health and diseases
- public policy and public affairs
- recreation, sports, and athletics
- religion, religious welfare, and religious education
- scholarships, student aid, and loans
- science and technology programs
- social and political science programs
- social services
- women and girls.

Over time, you will gain knowledge of the various resources available and be able to determine which are particularly valuable and worth purchasing for your nonprofit.

ETHICAL CONSIDERATIONS

When you engage in prospect research, give careful attention to ethical considerations. Information gathered about individuals, foundations, and corporations often is highly personal and should be treated with confidentiality and respect. We believe that you should adhere to the following guidelines:

+ Keep all your prospect research records confidential and in a secure place.
+ Use the records for your organization only; do not share prospect information or lists with other organizations.
+ Use only information sources that are available to the public.
+ Verify, verify, and verify information to the best of your ability.
+ Do not include embarrassing or irrelevant information in your records or on your prospect tracking reports.

All staff and volunteers who will be involved in researching prospects or in cultivation and solicitation must be apprised of and agree to such standards.

REFERENCES

Dun & Bradstreet. (1996). *Million dollar directory.* New York: Author.

Feczko, M. M. (Ed.). (1996). *The foundation directory—1996 edition.* New York: The Foundation Center.

The Foundation Center. (1996). *FC search: The Foundation Center's database on CD-ROM.* New York: Author.

Heller, J. (1996, June). Get the real story from SEC filings for free. *SmartMoney,* 5(6), 38–40.

Jenkins, J. B., & Lucas, M. (1985). *How to find philanthropic prospects.* Ambler, PA: Fund-Raising Institute.

Kaplan, A. E. (Ed.). (1996). *Giving USA—1996.* New York: AAFRC Trust for Philanthropy.

McGraw-Hill. (1996). *Standard and Poor's registry* (Vols. 1, 2, & 3). New York: Author.

Shirley, A. G. (1996). *North Carolina giving.* Raleigh, NC: Capital Consortium.

Wright, J. W. (1996). *The American almanac of jobs and salaries.* New York: Avon Books.

CHAPTER 5

SPECIAL EVENTS

Most nonprofits engage in some type of special event fundraising. Special events, or benefits, take on many forms—from doughnut sales to car washes, golf outings to black tie dinner dances, small raffles to major auctions. For many small nonprofits, special event work is their primary fundraising method. Although special events can be successful vehicles to raise funds, some potential pitfalls exist.

This chapter considers the rationale for conducting special event fundraisers, the costs of such events, factors to consider in deciding to engage in special events, factors involved in planning such events, and tax implications for your nonprofit and your donors.

SPECIAL EVENTS HAVE MULTIPLE PURPOSES

Before your nonprofit attempts to raise funds through special events, your board and staff should consider several things:
+ an analysis of the reasons for conducting the special event
+ the resources required to stage a successful event
+ the costs involved.

Confusion often exists about the purpose of special events. Special events may be used to raise money. They may be primarily a public relations vehicle. Most of the time, however, special events have multiple purposes. These purposes should be fully understood by nonprofit executives and board members.

Most fundraising professionals and nonprofit executives agree with Randall (1993) that special events should do the following:

- raise money
- provide an opportunity for people to have fun and possibly become involved with your organization ("friend-raising")
- help you reach people you might not reach otherwise
- call attention to your organization, cause, or project (p. 15).

Too often, nonprofits embark on special event fundraising without having completed a comprehensive fundraising plan, without setting funding goals for the event, and without a clear understanding of the real costs involved, including the commitment of staff and volunteer time necessary to make the event successful. Ideally, when your nonprofit engages in special event fundraising, you will strike a balance between the goals of raising money and increasing your organization's visibility. As Klein (1994) correctly points out

> An organization that simply needs money (perhaps from being in a cash flow bind, or having an unexpected expense) will find that the slowest ways to raise money are by proposal writing or having an event. On the other hand, a nonprofit that wants to raise its profile, bring in new people, and perhaps make some money immediately will find a special event an ideal strategy. (p. 97)

When embarking on special event fundraising, you should consider the extent to which the event will promote greater visibility for your nonprofit; at the same time, you should consider whether the proposed event will be cost-effective. The goal of using a special event as a vehicle to promote people having fun and possibly becoming involved in your nonprofit is laudable. However, this goal is not always consistent with raising money. Nonprofits sometimes make the mistake of aiming their special event at the wrong audience to raise money. That is, the pricing of the event is pegged at a level that will enable the organization's clients to participate but not at a level where significant amounts of money can be raised. Being clear about the purpose of the event will help you avoid such inconsistencies.

Using special events to call attention to your nonprofit is a worthwhile goal. If you are successful, you may enhance your nonprofit's visibility and raise its profile in your community. Because media coverage of your special event is often possible, a special event can be an excellent way to get your nonprofit's name and message before the public. However, if your primary goal is to raise the visibility of your nonprofit, strategies other than special events may be more cost-effective.

THE COSTS OF SPECIAL EVENTS

Many nonprofit fundraisers will agree with Randall's (1993) contention that, "Special events are a high cost method of fund raising" (p. 16). The costs generally fall into three categories: direct, indirect, and opportunity.

Direct costs of an event are perhaps the easiest to see and understand. Randall (1993) suggests that direct costs for special events typically are 25 percent to 50 percent of the gross revenue from the event. Direct costs may include mailings, facility rental, food, entertainment fees, and other essential items.

Indirect costs include the staff and volunteer time devoted to the event. These costs are less obvious and overlooking them can be a costly mistake. When the cost of staff time is calculated, you may often find that your special event is at best marginally profitable and at worst a money loser for your organization.

The opportunity cost of a special event is rarely considered by nonprofit executives and board members but often has a significant impact on your organization. Opportunity costs are losses in revenue and resources that result when you forego other profitable activities to invest your time and resources in an activity that rarely pays high dividends. Randall (1993) asserts that "the opportunity cost of the vast majority of special events is so high it makes them little more than poor quality 'loss leaders' " (p. 16).

You should consider whether the time and effort required to be successful in special event fundraising will generate greater returns for your nonprofit than if you invest in other types of fundraising activities.

THE POTENTIAL PITFALLS OF SPECIAL EVENTS

Although the costs alone may be sufficient to dissuade you from embarking on special events, you need to consider other potential pitfalls inherent in this method of fundraising.

One potential problem is that such events frequently require all participants to give the same amount of money, regardless of their personal financial circumstances or level of commitment to your cause. This practice tends to "flatten" giving to a lower level than what donors may, through other methods, be motivated to give. Special events "more often than not, succeed only in getting token gifts while leaving the donors with the impression they really did something meaningful to help and the mistaken notion their tokens were generous!" (Randall, 1993, p. 15).

Another problem with special events is that many fail to promote goodwill among your staff and volunteers. In many cases, they drain the energy and resources of your staff and volunteers who may have to spend a great deal of time selling tickets, securing gifts for auctions, or obtaining other types of support. The labor-intensive nature of activities involved in special event fundraising often leads to burnout among your volunteers and staff.

With special event fundraising, you also may reduce the effectiveness of other annual fund efforts. Donors may feel that through their participation in your special event they have "already contributed" to your nonprofit and may thus decline to give an annual gift, resulting in a decrease in overall revenue for your organization.

DECIDING TO ENGAGE IN SPECIAL EVENT FUNDRAISING

If your analysis of the costs and potential benefits of a special event leads you to conclude that the event will provide increased positive visibility for your nonprofit and bring in new money, then you should consider the following questions when undertaking a special event:

- What types of people are likely to support a special event?
- What type of event should your organization sponsor?

Klein (1994) suggests that two types of people attend events sponsored by nonprofit organizations: those who attend because of their interest in the event itself and those who are motivated both by the event and their interest in your organization. In the first category are individuals who may attend a road race, golf outing, or auction regardless of which organization sponsors the event. For fledgling nonprofits or those located in rural areas or small communities, events that generate support from "strangers" can be a highly productive strategy. The first category also includes businesses or corporations who may purchase advertisements in an event program book, donate auction or raffle prizes, buy tables at dinners or luncheons, sponsor holes at golf outings, or even sponsor the event itself. Many times, businesses who would otherwise not make a contribution to your organization will provide this type of support. Such support is a type of cause-related marketing that is discussed in greater detail in chapter 6.

The second category of special event participants—those who are both interested in your event and are interested in your organization or cause—may believe in your cause but may or may not know much about your organization. These individuals may find that your special event allows them to support a cause they believe in while they get something they want, such as playing golf at a prestigious course or obtaining a particular premium at an auction.

Our experience suggests that a third category of special events participants exists. These are individuals who already support your nonprofit. This category includes your board members, staff, volunteers, annual donors, others who are close to your organization, and sometimes clients or patrons. Analyze carefully the giving potential of this group. These individuals are your most likely supporters.

Klein (1994) has developed an excellent framework that nonprofit executives and board members can use in deciding on the type of special event fundraiser to launch. She suggests that you consider the following questions:

- How appropriate is the event for your organization?
- How will the event reflect on the image of your organization?
- How much volunteer time and energy will the event require?
- How much front money will be needed?
- How repeatable is the event and how does its timing fit?
- How does the event fit into your overall fundraising plan?

Is the Event Appropriate?

You should be concerned about how well the event reflects your nonprofit's mission and values. Will people who know nothing about your organization have positive or no worse than neutral feelings about your organization as the sponsor of the event? Or will you need to provide more explanation about your nonprofit to counter possible negative perceptions associated with your sponsorship of the event? If your situation is the latter, the event is probably inappropriate and you should consider a different type. Clearly, sponsorship of a wine tasting would be inappropriate for an alcohol treatment program as would sponsorship of a "Las Vegas Night" by a program that treats individuals with gambling, drug, and other addictions. Often, issues of appropriateness are more subtle than these examples and require careful consideration.

What Image Will the Event Give Your Nonprofit?

Related to determining the appropriateness of a particular event is considering whether the special event will promote an image of your nonprofit that is positive and with which you are comfortable. Some events that are appropriate for a particular nonprofit will not necessarily promote the kind of image you desire. For example, for many religious groups, raffles may fall into the category of events that do not promote a desirable image. Other examples of events that might be problematic are an expensive luncheon or dinner as a fundraiser for a homeless shelter or a raffle to raise money for an environmental group in which the prize is a vacation at an oceanfront resort. Like the issue of appropriateness, the image produced by an event, however subtle, requires careful thought.

How Many Volunteers Are Needed?

The amount of volunteer time and energy that will be required is a critical factor for most nonprofits. You should determine in advance how many people will be needed to run the event, what their tasks will be, and what time commitments will be required. You also must assess whether you have sufficient volunteers who are interested in and capable of doing the jobs that need to be done. Furthermore, you should assess whether you have sufficient staff to support your volunteers. Expect the unexpected. Nothing will serve you better than anticipating what may go awry. Finally, remember that you are using valuable volunteer resources. Ask yourself honestly whether your volunteers might be better used for something else.

How Much Money Is Needed in Advance?

Many types of special events require money up front, that is, funds to cover costs that accrue before revenues come in. Your board should be clearly informed about projected costs, and action should be taken to allocate funds for this purpose. A good rule to use in deciding whether to embark on a special event is to estimate carefully how much money your organization will lose if the event has to be canceled. Assess whether you can afford to absorb such a loss. Some special events require so much money up front that they create serious cash flow problems. Too often, nonprofits plunge headlong into special event fundraising without first calculating its real fiscal impact.

Can the Event Be Repeated?

Before embarking on a special event, some thought should be given to whether it is likely to be repeatable. Lack of repeatability alone should not rule out an event, but the prospect of being able to repeat an event, perhaps annually, is a positive factor. Repetition of events can lead to the establishment of important traditions. Participants will look forward to your annual event, whether it be a dinner dance, luncheon, road race, golf outing, or auction. As an added benefit, some savings of time and energy can be realized as procedures become routine. In addition, the publicity surrounding a special event often grows as the event becomes a regular and anticipated affair.

The matter of timing can be critical to the success or failure of your special event. To avoid conflicts that could prove fatal, be aware of holidays and other events in your community when scheduling your event. Be sure to be sensitive to multiethnic holidays and celebrations. As a courtesy and to avoid possible conflicts, notify similar organizations in your community once your event is scheduled.

Does the Event Fit Your Overall Fundraising Strategy?

Finally, you should consider your special event in light of your overall fundraising strategy or plan and institute a comprehensive evaluation. Ideally, your special event will generate positive publicity for your organization, program, or cause and generate funding from new sources. After each special event, conduct a careful, comprehensive evaluation so that you have a clear picture of the costs and benefits. Such an evaluation should include a detailed analysis of those who attended. Were they individuals who represent new donors to your organization or were they primarily your tried and true supporters? If the latter is the case, you may want to consider for them other less costly fundraising strategies.

PLANNING YOUR SPECIAL EVENT

Those people who have no experience in special event fundraising are often surprised to learn how much planning time is required to make such an event successful. Klein (1994) suggests that "Because so much can go wrong, and because many things often hinge on one thing so that one mistake can throw off weeks of work, events must be planned with more attention to minute details than almost any other fundraising strategy" (p. 101).

A special event is important to your nonprofit because of its visibility, commitment of volunteer and staff time, requirement for money up front, and potential for raising needed funds. Therefore, you must have in place an appropriate structure to plan and manage the event. Consider establishing a separate committee or task force, often a subcommittee of your board or fundraising steering committee, that will be responsible for planning and carrying out the event. Ideally, your special event committee chairperson will be a knowledgeable and energetic member of your board.

Clearly determine staff duties. Ideally, most of the work involved in putting on the special event will be done by your volunteers, because it is expensive to use your staff to organize an event. Nevertheless, you should identify staff support for the committee in advance and clearly articulate the expectations of staff vis-à-vis volunteers. Otherwise, you are likely to encounter logistical difficulties.

Primary responsibility for the overall planning of your event should rest with the special event committee. Ideally, your committee chairperson will serve as an effective link between the committee and your board of trustees. Keep the membership of your special event committee relatively small (for example, six to eight members) to help you stay focused on the tasks at hand. Keep in mind that the primary functions of your special event committee are planning and overall coordination. Beyond these functions, jobs and tasks related to the special event should be delegated to other volunteers.

Your special event committee, with appropriate staff support, should be charged with four principal tasks: developing an event master plan, preparing a budget, developing a time line, and evaluating the event.

An event master plan is a list of all the tasks and activities that must be accomplished in planning and conducting the event. The master plan should include all the minor, obvious tasks as well as the major tasks. In addition to listing each task, your master plan should indicate who will be responsible for accomplishing each task, when it should be accomplished, and the projected or budgeted cost. As each activity is completed, enter on the form the actual cost. Use of such a form will give you a good sense of whether you are staying within your budget. Figure 5-1 is an example of an event master plan form.

Your event budget should be realistic and comprehensive. The event master plan should indicate the items and activities that will involve costs, and your special event committee should prepare a budget that includes not only anticipated costs but also anticipated revenues. Klein's (1994) admonition about estimating costs is worth noting:

> As you budget, remember that an estimate is not a guess. If someone says, "The estimate for food is . . ." or " The estimate for printing is . . ." it means he or she has called several vendors for prices, bargained, and is satisfied that the estimate will be the price or very close to the price you will pay. (pp. 102–103)

FIGURE 5-1. SAMPLE SPECIAL EVENT MASTER PLAN FORM

Name of Event _____ Date of Event _____

Staff/Volunteer with Overall Responsibility_____

Task	Person Responsible	Date/Time Task to Be Completed	Projected Cost or Budget	Actual Cost
1.				
2.				
3.				
4.				
5.				
6.				
7.				
8.				
9.				
10.				

Once your budget is prepared, review it in relation to your master plan to determine the front costs that will be required and the impact that these costs may have on your nonprofit's cash flow. All of this fiscal information should go before your board of trustees for approval.

The next task for your committee is to prepare a time line. Create a chart on which you list the tasks and activities that need to be accomplished on the left side of the page and list units of time (days, weeks, or months) across the top of the page. For most special event planning, weeks are the most useful unit of time, although as you get closer to the event you may need to shift the time frame to days. Next to each task, place an "x" under the day, week, or month when the task must be accomplished. If the task will be accomplished over time, then you can place a mark at the starting and ending points and connect the marks. Your time line chart allows you to get a quick picture of where you are in your planning activities at any point. By referring to your time line, you can readily see whether your schedule has slipped, and by identifying such slippage early you can take appropriate steps to get back on track.

When determining time lines, look at the target date for the event and work backward. Determine as best as you can the amount of time needed to accomplish each task. Then, establish clear deadlines for completion.

You must have a plan for evaluating the success of your special event. Immediately after the event, carefully consider the following questions:

- Did the planning proceed according to your schedule?
- Did the event meet your goals both in terms of money and visibility?
- How did participants, volunteers, and staff regard the event?
- Did you stay within budget?
- What happened that was unanticipated?
- Did the event generate positive publicity?
- If you decide to repeat the event, what should you do differently?

This information is essential as you formulate plans to replicate the event or sponsor a different type of event.

Finally, document your activities and contacts every step of the way. You will need such a paper trail to thank everyone who assisted you. You will be surprised at the number of people you will need to thank—from the hotel receptionist who assisted event goers in finding your suite and the florist who "stretched" the flowers to accommodate additional last-minute tables to the volunteer who helped a participant with disabilities to her car and the board member who stayed late to help with clean up. Speedy and thoughtful acknowledgment will not only be genuinely appreciated, but also it will spread important goodwill for future events.

In addition, careful documentation of event activities and contacts will help you reconstruct the event should you decide to repeat it. Keep a good record of all important contact people and phone numbers, including your florist, printer, photographer, media contacts, catering company, and hotel.

Finally, although this may seem obvious, a task that is often overlooked is recording the names and addresses of all event participants. Include them on your routine and fundraising mailing lists. Remember, these individuals are your future donors!

TAX CONSIDERATIONS IN SPECIAL EVENTS

Your nonprofit should seek professional counsel from qualified attorneys and tax consultants regarding current IRS rules and regulations, but there are some general things about which you should be aware.

First, IRS substantiation and disclosure requirements, effective January 1, 1994, require that donors receive written acknowledgment from a charitable organization of gifts of $250 or more that are given as straight donations. These are gifts for which the donor received nothing of value in return. It is the donor's responsibility to obtain this documentation from the nonprofit; your nonprofit will not get into legal difficulty if it does not supply this information. Providing your donors with receipts or written documentation for all gifts is nevertheless a good practice. Often, such written documentation is simply a letter. At a minimum, the letter must note the amount of any cash the donor contributes. When gifts of property are donated, the documentation must include a description of the gift, but need not include a dollar value. In either case, the documentation should note that the donor did not receive any goods or services in return for or in consideration of the contribution.

Second, IRS requires that charities provide donors with written documentation when they have contributed more than $75 and have received some type of goods or services in return. Your nonprofit is required to provide this documentation and penalties exist for not providing it. This rule applies only to donated amounts of $75 or more. The written acknowledgment must inform the donor that only a part of the money that he or she contributed is tax deductible. The deductible amount is the total amount given minus the value of the goods or services received. Your nonprofit must provide the donor with a good-faith estimate of the value of the goods and services he or she received.

IRS does not allow a charitable deduction for money paid for a raffle ticket. Furthermore, if donations are made in return for tickets to some type of event, no deduction is allowed, regardless of whether the tickets are used. Thus, if a donor gives money and receives tickets to an event, only the excess amount over the value of the event is deductible, even if the tickets are not used.

If a donor buys an item at an auction or bazaar, the full amount paid is not considered deductible because the donor has received something of value. Even if the items sold at the auction or bazaar are given to the event at no charge, the total amount paid is not tax deductible. The items are still considered for tax purposes to have a fair market value. Consequently, the donor can take a charitable deduction only for the excess of the amount paid over the fair market value of the item or service purchased. However, those individuals or companies who donate such items to your nonprofit to be sold at an auction or bazaar may take a full charitable tax deduction.

You must keep a permanent, written record of your assessment of the fair market value of goods and services provided at your event. Because no specific formulas exist to make such determinations, it may be worthwhile to seek help from a volunteer who has experience in this area. For example, if a dinner or luncheon is served at an event, the fair market value is what someone would be charged for such a meal purchased in a restaurant, not what a caterer might charge your nonprofit for the meal. Similarly, if entertainment is provided during the event, you will need to assign a fair market value for this added perk. Because the valuation of entertainment is likely to be more subjective than the valuation of meals, gifts, or party favors, you should document carefully the process by which your special event committee arrived at a fair market value.

Because important legal and tax considerations are involved with special events, you should keep accurate information on all gifts, whether from participants or from those who provided goods or services used in the event. The North Carolina Community Foundation suggests the following information be kept:

- donor's or participant's name and an indication of whether the gift was in the form of cash or donated goods or services; include a formal name for mailing purposes (for example, Mrs. Jane Doe) and an appropriate name for the salutation of all communications (for example, Dear Jane or Dear Mrs. Doe)
- complete mailing address where acknowledgment should be sent
- amount of cash donations or description of donated goods or services
- whether the amount received from a donor was a true gift or if the donor was paying to participate in the special event fundraiser
- whether the payment from the donor was in cash or by check (if by check, be sure to record the check number)
- the fair market value of what the donor received, if anything, in return for the cash, goods, or services donated.

Using the information above, send acknowledgment letters to all participants in your special event as soon as possible after the event. The following is an example of wording to include in your thank you letter that addresses IRS regulations with regard to goods and services:

Please note that for tax purposes, the deductible portion of your gift is $ [the value of the contribution is the amount over the fair market value of goods or services received]. This amount represents the value of your gift minus the value of the [describe goods or services received by donor], which is valued at $ [value of goods or services]. Please keep this letter for your tax records.

EXAMPLES OF SUCCESSFUL SPECIAL EVENTS

Numerous nonprofits engage in successful special event fundraising activities, with the money raised varying from a few hundred to millions of dollars. Large national organizations are obviously positioned well to raise larger amounts of money through special events, whereas smaller, localized organizations may raise smaller amounts. The following are some examples of amounts raised by two national nonprofits through different types of special events:

- Over the 1996 Labor Day weekend, the Muscular Dystrophy Association raised $49.1 million from its annual telethon hosted by Jerry Lewis (Associated Press, 1996).
- At its fifth annual Race Against Breast Cancer in Chicago, the Y-ME National Breast Cancer Organization had more than 5,500 participants and raised approximately $400,000 (Y-ME National Breast Cancer Organization, 1996).

Below are some examples of successful fundraisers by state and local nonprofits:

- The PlayMakers Repertory Company of Chapel Hill (North Carolina) had 314 guests at its 1994 PlayMakers Ball, a New Orleans–themed black-tie dinner dance and raised approximately $100,000.
- At its 1994 Evening with Friends Gala, the AIDS Service Agency of Raleigh, North Carolina, raised $68,000 from more than 2,700 people who attended 101 separate dinner parties.
- The Cystic Fibrosis Foundation of Raleigh, North Carolina, raised $46,200 at The Tennis Auction, its 1994 black-tie dinner dance.
- An opening night black-tie gala celebrating the opening of a new collection of Old Masters paintings at the North Carolina Museum of Art raised $40,000.

- The American Lung Association Celebrity Waiters Dinner followed by a dance and auction, in Raleigh, North Carolina, raised $31,000.
- Interact of Raleigh, North Carolina, a nonprofit that provides safety and support for victims of domestic violence and survivors of rape and sexual assault, raised $27,000 from its Phantom Ball, in which guests purchased tickets for the privilege of *not attending* yet another fundraising party. Incidentally, the tickets also served to enter purchasers in a raffle for tickets for a four-day trip to London (Westarp, 1995).
- The Walker Home and School in Needham, Massachusetts, has used golf and tennis outings as successful fundraisers, raising more than $182,000 at Fore the Children, its 1996 golf event, and $101,000 at For the Children with Love, its 1996 tennis tournament.

Many different types of special events can be planned, all with varying degrees of fundraising potential. Select a type of event that is appropriate for your nonprofit, that you can afford both in terms of energy and front money, and that will be fun for those who participate either as patrons or volunteers. Paula Harris, co-chairperson of the 1996 Y-ME Race Against Breast Cancer, commented after the event, "Putting the race together took all the time, energy and enthusiasm we had, but standing on the stage, watching the sea of people going down Columbus Drive, gave it all back" (Y-ME National Breast Cancer Organization, 1996).

CONCLUSION

Special events can do many things for your nonprofit, including raising money. However, you should be clear about your goals and objectives before undertaking a special event and you should understand the various costs involved, including the opportunity costs.

Once you decide to embark on a special event, devote a significant amount of time and energy to planning. Be certain that you have in place adequate staffing and volunteer structures to make the event successful. Keep careful records of everything related to the event, be sure to thank everyone involved, and carefully evaluate the event's success in relation to your goals and the amount of effort involved. Then you will be in a good position to make an informed decision about whether to repeat your event. For more detailed information about specific types of special events, you may wish to consult some of the publications listed in appendixes A and C.

REFERENCES

Associated Press. (1996, September 3). Jerry Lewis telethon raises $49.1 million. *Raleigh (NC) News & Observer*, p. 2A.

Klein, K. (1994). *Fundraising for social change*. (3rd ed.). Inverness, CA: Chardon Press.

Randall, M. (1993, April). What you should know about special events. *Fund Raising Management*, pp. 15–16.

Westarp, P. E. (1995, January 3). Heartiest parties of '94. *Raleigh (NC) News & Observer*, pp. 1E–2E.

Y-ME National Breast Cancer Organization. (1996, July/August). Fifth annual race a huge success (p. 3). *Y-ME Hotline*. Chicago: Author.

CHAPTER 6

CAUSE–RELATED MARKETING

Corporate philanthropic support of nonprofit organizations in 1994 rose by 1 percent compared with the previous year. This minor increase continues a pattern of little change in corporate philanthropy over the previous 10 years. As reported in *Giving USA—1996* (Kaplan, 1996), corporate philanthropy totaled $7.4 billion in 1995, representing approximately 5.1 percent of all philanthropic giving. However, as a result of a rise in the number of companies supporting nonprofits through their marketing, advertising, public relations, community relations, or government relations departments, it is difficult to determine the total support corporate America provides.

Until the early 1950s, corporate giving was legally restricted to charities that were in some way connected to the activities of the business. The rationale was that management's primary responsibility was to shareholders. As a result of court rulings during the 1950s, this restriction was eliminated, and corporate support of nonprofits, especially those involved with arts and education, increased significantly. During the early 1980s, corporate philanthropy experienced dramatic increases. At the same time, increased demands were placed on companies' charitable activities. Deep cuts in government funding for a wide array of social programs resulted in many nonprofits finding themselves in a more competitive fundraising environment. "Cut off from government funds . . . nonprofit organizations found themselves scrambling to fill a financial vacuum. Corporate America—supposed to benefit from Reagan's changes—seemed a logical place to go fundraising" (Zetlin, 1990, p. 10). Consequently, companies, especially visible and profitable ones, were flooded with funding requests.

During this same period, however, many companies were confronted with numerous business challenges, including foreign competition, emerging opportunities in international markets, changes in technology, and shareholder pressure to improve profitability. These challenges, coming at the same time corporate America was being asked to respond with unprecedented generosity, raised new questions concerning philanthropic priorities and decision making. Companies began to rethink their charitable giving, factoring into their philanthropic decision making consideration of the business benefits accrued from their giving. As noted by Dienhart (1988), the "emerging strategy [was] to treat donations like investments and to expect some return from them" (p. 64). This approach, labeled "strategic giving" by Zetlin (1990), meant giving with an eye on the business corporation's eventual best interests. This notion of enlightened self-interest is a critical one that is at the core of the changing paradigm of corporate philanthropy in the 1990s.

In their book, *Companies with a Conscience*, Scott and Rothman (1992) discuss the extent to which enlightened self-interest can serve corporate objectives. Their study of 12 companies with strong records of profitability and philanthropy suggests that the issue often is one of short-term versus long-term strategies:

> These companies have made related decisions that had a negative impact on their bottom lines in the short-term. But the enduring nature of these businesses and the fact that every one of their products and services remains heavily in demand in an almost cultlike fashion, shows that their long-term vision was correct. (p. 209)

Ben and Jerry's Ice Cream, one of the 12 companies featured by Scott and Rothman, operates as a profitable business while maintaining an unwavering commitment to a wide spectrum of social causes. We believe that this commitment to product quality and social responsibility is the driving force in making a company more profitable and philanthropic than other companies.

Another example of strategic giving is reflected in IBM's philanthropy in recent years. Despite record financial losses, IBM has donated millions of dollars in computer equipment each year. This strategy is considered simply good business. As noted by Fisch (1992), whether sales are down or business is booming, "corporate grantmakers are becoming more focused on strategic giving, the art of meshing community needs with corporate interests and identifying ways in which grants can make the most impact" (p. 6).

CAUSE–RELATED MARKETING: DEFINITIONS AND CRITICISMS

An increasing number of companies are using cause-related marketing as a key component of their overall plan for strategic giving (Hemphill, 1996). Cause-related marketing is a form of partnership between companies and nonprofit organizations. These partnership arrangements frequently are referred to as "cause marketing," "social responsibility marketing," "joint promotional marketing," "joint venture marketing," or "public purpose marketing."

Although various definitions of cause-related marketing have been offered since American Express registered the term in the early 1980s, all definitions emphasize the establishment of mutually beneficial relationships between corporations and nonprofits in which the former pursues marketing and promotional objectives while the latter pursues fundraising and public relations objectives. File and Prince (1995) point out that "The usual objectives of cause-related marketing programs are to raise incremental funds for the nonprofit's cause and to promote the image and products of the business sponsor" (p. 249). Garrison (1990) notes that for nonprofits, cause-related marketing "offer[s] new sources of financial support and increased public exposure. Both are important in a fund-raising arena that grows more and more competitive. For corporate partners, cause-related marketing provides an opportunity to increase product sales, gain public recognition and, at the same time, support the causes they care about" (p. 40).

Although cause-related marketing is increasing, critics charge that the concept is flawed and that a charitable contribution should not provide the donor with a profit. Gurin (1987) charges that cause-related marketing efforts frequently help causes that likely need such funding the least. Kotler and Andreasen (1991) suggested that the public might develop negative attitudes both toward the company and the selected charity because of dissatisfaction with these kinds of partnerships. Other criticisms frequently voiced in nonprofit circles include concern that cause-related marketing will erode traditional corporate philanthropy, that individuals will perceive they are making their charitable donations through their purchases of products from companies involved in cause-related marketing, that the time-limited nature of these partnership arrangements will leave the nonprofit organization with a major revenue shortfall when the cause-related marketing activity is completed, or that the nonprofit will experience severe image problems if the wrong business partner is selected. Notwithstanding these criticisms, in an environment that requires nonprofits to diversify their revenue streams and seek new strategic alliances, cause-related marketing opportunities are being aggressively pursued.

EXAMPLES OF CAUSE-RELATED MARKETING

The concept of cause-related marketing encompasses a wide variety of potential partnership arrangements between companies and nonprofit organizations. The following represent some of the most frequently used approaches:

- credit card purchase or use linked to particular social causes
- sponsorship of special events (one-time or ongoing)
- product endorsements, promotions, and sales, including coupon redemption
- product licensing arrangements.

Some companies also include in-kind goods and services as an integral part of their cause-related marketing partnerships. Whatever the strategic approach, businesses and nonprofits enter into agreements linking publicity, sales, fundraising, and in some situations, volunteerism, so that both for-profit and nonprofit objectives can be achieved. As indicated in the examples that follow, cause-related marketing may assume a variety of partnership arrangements.

American Express

The American Express Company agreed to support the restoration of the Statue of Liberty financially by donating $1 each time a new American Express card was issued in the United States. Furthermore, the company agreed to donate 1¢ for restoration efforts each time an American Express card was used to purchase an item. This linking of the corporation's profit objectives with a nonprofit mission and activity during a specified time period resulted in a 45 percent increase in the number of cards issued and a 28 percent increase in card usage, providing a significant increase in revenue for American Express. The company contributed $1.7 million to the restoration effort.

Sierra Club

The Sierra Club, with a membership in excess of 500,000, established an affinity group marketing program in partnership with Chase Lincoln First Bank of Rochester, New York. Sierra Club members are targeted to apply for and use a credit card issued only to its members. In one year, the Sierra Club received $225,000 in revenue from this cause-related marketing activity.

Multiple Sclerosis Association, Lupus Foundation of America, and United States Rowing Association

The Multiple Sclerosis Association, the Lupus Foundation of America, and the United States Rowing Association entered into an agreement with Flowers Direct, a long-distance floral service that connects customers with independent florists. These organizations receive a donation for each call placed on a designated toll-free number; the amount of the contribution was determined by each organization's membership size and its ability to participate in the Flowers Direct program.

NAACP

The National Association for the Advancement of Colored People (NAACP) provides TransNational Communications, Inc., with the names and addresses of its 650,000 members and supporters. Trans-National markets its long-distance service to this group at a reduced rate, and NAACP receives a percentage of all monthly payments generated by new subscribers.

Metropolitan Opera

When Chanel wanted to reach wealthy, influential New Yorkers to launch a new perfume, it selected the Metropolitan Opera as a partner. Chanel sponsored an opening night fundraising dinner and fashion show, and both partners profited. The Met received $1.2 million in donations in a short period, and Chanel reached its target audience.

Museum of Science and Industry

When Chrysler launched its new "Eagle Vision" automobile in 1993, it gave the Museum of Science and Industry in Tampa, Florida, $20,000 in exchange for the museum displaying the car and keeping it clean for museum goers.

Second Harvest Food Bank Network

Pillsbury and Super Valu used coupon redemption promotions in an effort to increase sales and to support the Second Harvest Food Bank Network. They realized a 46 percent increase in sales, and Second Harvest received a $22,000 donation.

Feed the Children

Boisset USA, the U.S. division of an international wine company, produces and sells high-quality, affordable wines while helping to reduce hunger among American children. Through an agreement with the Oklahoma-based Feed the Children Campaign, 10 percent of gross sales profit on specific wines was contributed to the nonprofit. Through the use of point-of-sale campaigns, donation boxes, and restaurant "table tents" to increase wine sales, Boisset USA contributed sufficient financial support to provide 2.8 million meals annually.

Mirabella

The magazine *Mirabella* told its advertisers that for every advertising page in its first anniversary issue, $1,000 would go to one of four charities, including an AIDS foundation. The magazine raised $82,000 for the nonprofit organizations and increased the number of advertising pages in that issue.

National Audubon Society

The National Audubon Society, a 500,000-member-strong organization with environmental advocacy as a central part of its mission, licenses its name to Bushnell to be used in the company's production and marketing of its binoculars, to MCI for an affinity telephone program, to Glidden Paint as part of a rebate program, and to a number of book publishers. For the use of its name, the society receives funding and public relations support.

Arthritis Foundation

Johnson & Johnson's McNeil Consumer Products Company (producer of Tylenol) has an arrangement with the Arthritis Foundation to jointly market a line of pain relief pills that bear the name of the nonprofit—Arthritis Foundation Pain Reliever. This arrangement guarantees the Arthritis Foundation a minimum of $1 million annually for the use of its name. In addition, each box of pills will include information about the services of the Arthritis Foundation, a free one-year membership application form, a complimentary subscription to *Arthritis Today*, and a toll-free number users can call for additional information about the foundation.

The examples listed in the previous paragraphs are illustrative of the various forms of cause-related marketing. Through such partnerships, nonprofits can receive substantial support, and businesses can stand out from the competition, enhance their public image, and make a profit. Whether the goal is targeting a new market, launching a new product, or increasing sales, a partnership with a nonprofit can have multiple benefits.

MAGNITUDE OF CAUSE–RELATED MARKETING

How many businesses and nonprofits are engaged in cause-related marketing is not known. The competitive nature of business, the blurring of cause-related marketing efforts with traditional philanthropy, and limited reporting requirements make it difficult to determine the numbers of businesses, nonprofits, and amount of funds involved. Although its magnitude cannot be stated with certainty, cause-related marketing will almost certainly increase as a method to create mutually beneficial relationships between companies and nonprofits. A number of studies offer findings that support this conclusion.

In 1988 Independent Sector commissioned a study of cause-related marketing practices of 17 corporations and 13 nonprofit organizations. Corporations were selected from beverage and food, packaged goods, financial, entertainment, and pharmaceutical industries. Among the nonprofits were health and human services organizations, emergency relief agencies, and cultural organizations. The study focused on attitudes of nonprofit professionals and corporate executives, the relationship of cause-related marketing to corporate philanthropy programs, applications, success factors, and effectiveness issues. The survey reported generally positive responses about the concept of and experiences with the varied approaches to cause-related marketing. Although challenges occurred meeting tight deadlines, facing communication problems, and addressing decision-making issues, the survey concluded that most for-profit and nonprofit respondents foresaw continued growth of the use of cause-related marketing.

The study by Barnes (1991), in which 25 corporate marketing executives and 23 fundraising managers participated, reported similar findings. Using a random sampling procedure, Barnes selected 50 companies from the Fortune 500 list and 50 nonprofit organizations from a list of the country's largest charities published by the Better Business Bureau. Barnes considered concerns, benefits, risks, and outlook associated with cause-related marketing. She reported that the majority of corporate representatives (70 percent) and nonprofit fundraising managers (73 percent) agreed on the likelihood that cause-related marketing (joint venture campaigns in Barnes' reference) will increase in popularity during the 1990s. This positive outlook is premised on the perceived benefits that accrue to both corporations and nonprofit organizations. Barnes reported that neither corporations nor nonprofits thought cause-related marketing would become a substitute for corporate philanthropy. Her study yielded findings that corporations

> appear to be more cautious about pursuing cause-related marketing campaigns than their nonprofit counterparts. They judge there is a risk involved and some logistical difficulties in dealing with the bureaucratic structure of nonprofit organizations. They also are more likely to agree that nonprofits are the compromising party and the most at risk in a joint venture marketing campaign. (p. 85)

Cone Communications (1993), via a study commissioned with Roper Starch Worldwide, focused the spotlight on cause-related marketing from a different perspective—that of potential business customers (consumers). Interviews with 1,981 people clearly established a positive relationship between consumer buying habits and companies' attempts to show their involvement in charitable causes. One of the survey's most surprising findings was the strength of corporate social responsibility as a reason people gave when asked what they considered when buying brands. The results indicated that approximately two-thirds of study participants were somewhat likely or very likely to switch brands "based on a good cause."

Consumers' consideration of corporate social responsibility is now in the second tier of important purchase influences. Although past experience, price, and quality are still the most important influences in consumer purchasing, the results of this survey provide solid empirical support for advocates of cause-related marketing. During the 1980s, many Americans were seeking luxury and prestige, and they bought products that fulfilled that aspiration. However, the study results suggest that to succeed during the 1990s products must meet more than just the price and quality demands of consumers. Consumers want to believe that their purchasing behaviors reflect their personal values.

A study by File and Prince (1995) of more than 400 medium-sized (50 to 500 employees) nonprofit arts organizations in New York, New Jersey, and Connecticut led to the conclusion that

> Commitment to cause-related marketing programs is not a phenomenon restricted to the largest corporations in the United States. . . [and that] at least one-fifth of medium-size businesses in the sample actively sought to promote themselves, or their goods and services, through their charitable contributions to nonprofits. (p. 258)

File and Prince further suggest "that managed well, cause-related marketing represents a new opportunity for resource development for nonprofits" (p. 259).

Two additional, more anecdotal indicators offer persuasive evidence that cause-related marketing will continue to grow in importance. The first of these indicators is the practice by some advertising and public relations firms to offer cause-related marketing assistance to their business clientele as part of the array of services provided. The second indicator is the emergence of for-profit businesses (for example, the International Events Group and JAMI Charity Brands) whose primary business is assisting companies in their cause-related marketing activities. These for-profit organizations offer services ranging from identifying potential partners to assuming extensive responsibility for planning and implementing companies' cause-related marketing initiatives.

SELECTION OF CAUSE-RELATED MARKETING PARTNERS

Numerous studies have underscored the critical importance of selecting an appropriate partner for cause-related marketing (Barnes, 1991; Independent Sector, 1988; Yankey, 1993). Criteria used by corporations in selecting partners frequently include the following for the nonprofit:

+ offering a conceptual, target market, or image link with the company or product
+ being well respected in terms of cause and integrity of governance and management

- being well known and highly visible
- having a national organizational base with extensive grassroots
- having a compelling issue that captures public attention
- possessing the potential for being a unique link for the company
- having performed successfully in prior cause-related marketing ventures
- being noncontroversial.

Other important considerations in companies' selection of nonprofit partners include the following:

- extent of exclusive sponsorship afforded
- nonprofit support elements available
- degree of control granted to corporate leaders
- synergy with other marketing and advertising efforts of the corporation.

Many of these same criteria are equally important for nonprofit organizations as they consider for-profit partners. Nonprofits seek corporate partners that have the following qualities:

- a conceptual, target market, or image link with the mission of the nonprofit
- a public image of being stable and well managed
- a well-known, positive company reputation
- a noncontroversial history.

In addition, nonprofits often include the following criteria in their deliberations:

- benefits for organizational clientele or members
- amount of staff time required
- willingness and capacity of the company to provide people and product support
- amount of public awareness that can be generated
- potential to increase the nonprofit organization's name recognition
- anticipated out-of-pocket costs and staffing requirements of the proposal
- degree of autonomy afforded by the company
- potential to recruit new volunteers or acquire new consumers
- increased attendance at events by volunteers.

The bottom line in selecting cause-related marketing partners is to match the cause and the product. Both the companies and nonprofits must carefully research prospective partners to ensure that the respective corporate cultures and objectives are compatible.

KEY SUCCESS FACTORS IN CAUSE-RELATED MARKETING

Companies and nonprofits frequently cite the following factors as contributing to the success of cause-related marketing efforts:

- a high level of awareness about the project among employees and consumers
- careful planning and contracting to identify and clarify what is involved in the marketing exchange
- integrity and follow-through by the company managers, nonprofit board, executive director, and project manager
- simplicity.

Companies report that when problems do arise, the most frustrating experiences usually are related to first-time participation in cause-related marketing activities. At the base of these problems often is gaining approval through the designated line of authority and making sure that all departments and product line managers sign off on the negotiated agreement or contract.

Frequent communication and organizational follow-through by the nonprofit partner are cited often as other key success factors. Businesses want to build relationships with their nonprofit partners and view frequent communication as essential to achieving that expected outcome. This communication should include progress reports, details on promotional efforts, potential problems, and changes in plans of action or time tables. Companies seek to avoid cause-related marketing partnerships wherein

- nonprofits fail to deliver functionally what was contractually established
- excessive amounts of volunteer staffing are required of the companies
- tight deadlines preclude adequate planning.

In summary, success seems directly related to selection of an appropriate partner, early clarification of goals and objectives of both partners, commitment of sufficient financial and human resources, frequent communication, and written agreements or contracts.

Most frequently, a company's decision to become involved in cause-related marketing partnerships is determined by a product or marketing manager. Obviously, the president or chief executive officer is an important actor, but decision making often is decentralized to product or marketing departments. In some businesses, managers of corporate philanthropic programs are included in decision making. In nonprofit organizations, decision-making authority for entering cause-related marketing partnerships most frequently resides with the executive director. In some nonprofits, the decision-making authority is shared with the executive committee of the board of directors (or trustees) or with fundraising and marketing staff.

Companies and nonprofit organizations have developed a number of outcomes to measure the degree of success of cause-related marketing activities. Clearly, an expectation of win–win outcomes exists, that is, outcomes wherein both parties perceive they have achieved their individual goals. Beyond this overall expectation, cause-related marketing projects require articulation of specific performance indicators or outcomes. These indicators or outcomes will be incorporated in the agreements or contracts established to guide the partnership arrangement. Examples of such indicators or outcomes include the following:

- product or service sales increase in a defined period
- volume of coupon redemption
- television market penetration
- media coverage (newspapers, magazines, radio, and television)
- attendees at events (numbers, potential consumers, and so forth)
- employee volunteerism
- dollars generated for nonprofit mission and activities
- distribution increase in educational and public awareness materials
- perceived "fun" reported by employees, customers, and donors
- perceived enthusiasm for cause-related marketing project.

In short, both companies and nonprofits must be clear regarding their respective outcome expectations. Cause-related marketing agreements and contracts must encompass these expectations and offer sufficient direction to enable all parties to measure the full range of benefits of the partnership arrangement.

CAUSE–RELATED MARKETING AGREEMENTS

Because cause-related marketing is a mutually beneficial business exchange and not traditional philanthropic support, both companies and nonprofits should have formal, written agreements or contracts to guide their partnership. Although the specific elements of an agreement or contract will depend on the nature of the cause-related marketing arrangements, written agreements should be made clarifying the following:

- specific products and timetable for activities to be conducted
- advertising approvals
- use of the nonprofit organization's name and logo
- specific financial support (how much, how paid, when distributed) to be received by the nonprofit organization
- steps to be pursued in the event of disagreements or unanticipated results
- sponsorship rights and fees
- termination of agreement
- posttermination rights
- indemnification
- confidentiality.

Some states have laws that require cause-related marketing agreements or contracts to have specific elements; these laws must be adhered to in developing any agreements or contracts. You should have an attorney review your cause-related marketing contracts before obligating your organization.

In addition to legally required elements, companies may have a number of financial goals for each cause-related marketing arrangement undertaken. These goals will not be incorporated into the agreements or contracts but will be used by companies both to guide their participation and to judge the success of the program. Likewise, you should have specific goals for your nonprofit. These goals may include awareness building, increased publicity, volunteer involvement, and expectations about funds to be raised. Such goals will guide your participation and can be used to judge success from the perspective of your organization.

CONCLUSION

Smith (1993), reflecting on the maturity of corporate giving and its long-term consequences, posited that

> Corporate managers now view the welfare of the corporation as inextricably tied to the health of the rest of society. . . . The maturity of corporate giving, therefore, has very specific implications for those seeking corporate support. The most important of these is the imperative of recognizing that the motives behind corporate giving are so much related to philanthropy as to enlightened self-interest. Any hope of developing a support relationship must be based on an understanding of this self-interest. . . . Once a support relationship has been established, charitable organizations must therefore keep their corporate donors informed about the successes, and failures, of their ongoing efforts. . . . In a nutshell, charitable organizations must recognize and understand what the maturity of corporate giving means. To effectively pursue the corporate dollar, they must have an equivalent maturity in their dealings with the corporate community. (pp. 226–227)

Although Smith's conclusions are directed toward nonprofits' understanding and appreciation of corporate philanthropy, the notions expressed are well suited to cause-related marketing. As indicated earlier, cause-related marketing activities represent corporate enlightened self-interest potentially at its best. When appropriate partners engage in cause-related marketing guided by clearly articulated agreements or contracts, evidence indicates that both businesses and nonprofit organizations emerge as clear winners. In developing your nonprofit's corporate giving strategies, you should view cause-related marketing as an opportunity to inform and educate selected corporations about a variety of issues that otherwise may never be explored by those corporations.

At the present, no evidence exists to suggest that cause-related marketing programs have contributed to any demise of corporate philanthropy. Rather, those factors that are contributing to the "flattening" of corporate giving appear to be part of the much larger reconfiguring and re-engineering occurring in the for-profit sector. Cause-related marketing has provided and will continue to provide a creative and financially feasible avenue for corporate America to support nonprofit organizations.

REFERENCES

Barnes, N. G. (1991). Philanthropy, profits, and problems: The emergence of joint venture marketing. *Akron Business and Economic Review, 22*(4), 78–86.

Cone Communications. (1993). *The Cone/Roper study: A benchmark survey of consumers' awareness and attitudes toward cause related marketing.* Boston: Author.

Dienhart, J. W. (1988). Charitable investments: A strategy for improving the business environment. *Journal of Business Ethics, 7*(1/2), 63–71.

File, K. M., & Prince, R. A. (1995). Cause-related marketing, philanthropy, and the arts. *Nonprofit Management & Leadership, 5*(2), 249–260.

Fisch, J. (1992, June). Recession hits corporate funders hardest of all grantmakers. *The Nonprofit Times*, pp. 1, 6.

Garrison, J. R. (1990). A new twist to cause marketing. *Fund Raising Management, 20*(12), 40–44.

Gurin, M. (1987). Don't rush into cause-related marketing. *NSFRE Journal*, 49.

Hemphill, T. A. (1996). Cause-related marketing, fundraising, and environmental nonprofit organizations. *Nonprofit Management and Leadership, 6*(4), pp. 403–418.

Independent Sector. (1988). *Study of cause-related marketing.* Washington, DC: Author.

Kaplan, A. E. (Ed.).(1996). *Giving USA—1996.* New York: AAFRC Trust for Philanthropy.

Kotler, P., & Andreasen, A. (1991). *Strategic marketing for nonprofit organizations* (4th ed.). Englewood Cliffs, NJ: Prentice Hall.

Scott, M., & Rothman, H. (1992). *Companies with a conscience: Intimate portraits of twelve firms that make a difference.* New York: Carol Publishing Group.

Smith, H. (1993). The maturity of corporate giving and its long-term consequences. *Nonprofit Management & Leadership, 4*(2), 215–228.

Yankey, J. A. (1993). *Cause related marketing among Cleveland's corporations and
nonprofit organizations.* Unpublished manuscript, Case Western Reserve
University, Mandel Center for Nonprofit Organizations, Cleveland, OH.

Zetlin, M. (1990). Companies find profit in corporate giving. *Management
Review, 79*(12), 10–15.

CHAPTER 7

PUTTING IT ALL TOGETHER: AN OVERVIEW

Fundraising is a process, not a science. It takes time, commitment, and resources, and it demands the best in us. A fundraiser wears many hats and simultaneously juggles many tasks and demands. This role requires both great organizational and people skills. Above all, it requires integrity and a sincere commitment to putting the needs of the donor first.

Meaningful giving can make a dream happen for someone, can offer a family an opportunity to memorialize a loved one, leave an important family legacy, or truly make a difference in the lives of others. It can make a lasting impression on one's life.

A high level of flexibility, responsiveness, and persistence is critical to successful fundraising. You also must recognize the two essential elements of fundraising: (1) people give to people, and (2) people give because they are asked. Personal relationships are at the center of all successful fundraising. These relationships must be nurtured or cultivated often over a long period.

You must base your fundraising success not only on the financial goals achieved but also on how well you increase the visibility and credibility of your nonprofit and on how effective you are in identifying and motivating donors and "matching" their interests with giving opportunities. Most important, you should measure your success by how well your nonprofit develops meaningful and mutually beneficial relationships with individual, foundation, and corporate supporters.

To ensure your nonprofit's survival, you must build a strong financial foundation that attracts an increasing base of supporters. A strong emphasis on fundraising activities that are well planned and multifaceted is critical. Attention must be given and adequate resources devoted to identifying and cultivating a network of individual, corporate, and foundation donors, particularly those with major gift potential.

Nonprofit fundraisers must be aware that people give for multiple and complex reasons. Involving potential donors in meaningful ways with your organization is essential, as is making regular and thoughtful requests for support. Individuals who volunteer with your nonprofit are more likely to contribute and to contribute at higher levels. Also important is a strong belief in the mission of your organization. Involvement can lead to increased knowledge about your organization and a greater belief in your cause.

Successful fundraising by nonprofits in the years ahead also will depend on your recognition of and well-planned responses to changing demographics. You must identify, reach out to, and involve individuals who may not have traditionally been involved in philanthropy. In particular, this strategy means greater involvement with Hispanic people, African American people, Asian American people and women. You also must be alert to unique giving patterns of prospect subgroups, such as baby boomers, and changing economic trends and conditions.

The process of successful fundraising is inherently multifaceted. A blend of strategies that includes major gift activity as well as regular annual fund appeals is needed. A fundraising plan that is truly comprehensive also will include elements of planned giving, special events, and cause-related marketing strategies. However, your nonprofit should approach a planned-giving program only with adequate expertise and legal assistance and special events with clear objectives and safeguards. The same is true for cause-related marketing strategies. Although cause-related marketing may look like a promising fundraising strategy for nonprofits that is likely to grow in significance in the future, specific experience or expertise and wise counsel is needed to be successful. In all cases, remember that financial support should be sought from a diverse donor base including individuals, corporations, and foundations.

Before launching a fundraising program or campaign, you should engage in an assessment of internal and external organizational readiness. You must first determine whether your board is sufficiently diverse and strong enough to support a fundraising effort as well as whether your nonprofit has adequate resources of staff, time, and money to engage in fundraising. You must then assess, among others things, whether your community is likely to support your fundraising effort and the degree of competition with other organizations.

Put together staff and volunteer structures that support fundraising by establishing a special committee of your board or creating other committees or councils to support your efforts. The widely used gift pyramid can then help you determine a realistic yet ambitious fundraising goal.

An essential tool in fundraising is your case for support. The case for support is a statement or document that explains your nonprofit's funding needs and motivates the reader to give. The importance of the case cannot be overstated. Great care should be given to preparing a succinct, attractive, and compelling document.

Finally, your fundraising efforts will be made easier if they are based on solid prospect research. Good research will provide you with information about prospects' interests and giving potential. This information is key to developing effective cultivation and solicitation strategies.

If you carefully identify prospective donors who have the capacity to make gifts and an established interest in your cause, involve them in meaningful ways with your nonprofit, and provide them with appropriate and thoughtful opportunities to give, you will more often than not experience success. In fundraising, success tends to breed additional success. Keep in mind that fundraising is a process that takes time. If you approach the process in a well-planned manner and if you devote adequate time and other resources to implementing your efforts, you will no doubt build a strong foundation that will support your nonprofit well into the future.

RESOURCES FOR NONPROFIT FUNDRAISERS

The following is a list of organizations, periodicals, and books that we have found helpful to us in our fundraising activities.

Organizations

American Association of Fund-Raising Counsel (AAFRC)
25 West 43rd Street, Suite 820
New York, NY 10036
212-354-5799

This is an organization of professional fundraising firms that helps nonprofits plan and manage fundraising programs, studies trends in American philanthropy, and annually publishes *Giving USA* as well as the bimonthly newsletter, *The Fund Raising Review*.

Center for Community Change
1000 Wisconsin Avenue, NW
Washington, DC 20007
202-342-0519
http://www.pratt.edu/picced/resource/ccc.html

This organization assists local groups, especially organizations assisting low-income populations and racial and ethnic groups, with planning and organizational development as well as with fundraising.

Council for Advancement and Support of Education (CASE)
11 Dupont Circle, Suite 400
Washington, DC 20036
202-328-5900
http://www.case.org

This is an organization of educational institutions that provides professional development opportunities for fundraising professionals in education.

Council on Foundations
1828 L Street, NW, Suite 300
Washington, DC 20036
202-466-6512

This is a membership organization of various types of foundations, corporate grantmakers, and trust companies that seeks to promote responsible and effective grantmaking as well as to encourage collaboration among grantmakers and promote the formation of new foundations. It publishes the bimonthly *Foundation News* and other useful publications.

The Foundation Center
79 Fifth Avenue
New York, NY 10003-3076
212-620-4230
http://fdncenter.org

This organization, which is primarily supported by foundations, provides a range of valuable information about grants through its publications and national network of resource libraries. Its publications include the *Foundation Directory, Foundation Grants Index, Foundation Center National Data Book*, and it offers computer search services. For more information, see appendix B.

The Grantsmanship Center
1125 West Sixth Street, 5th Floor
Los Angeles, CA 90017
213-482-9860
http://www.tgci.com

This is a national training organization that conducts workshops across the country on grantwriting, program management, fundraising, and other topics of relevance to nonprofits. It also produces a number of publications of value to nonprofits, including *The Grantsmanship Center Magazine* and *The Grantsmanship Center Whole Nonprofit Catalog.*

Independent Sector
1828 L Street, NW
Washington, DC 20036
202-223-8100
http://www.indepsec.org

This organization is made up of national voluntary organizations, foundations, and corporations with major philanthropic programs. It works to enhance giving, volunteering, and nonprofit initiatives.

National Center for Nonprofit Boards
2000 L Street, NW, Suite 510
Washington, DC 20036-4907
202-452-6262
1-800-883-6262
gopher://ncnb.org:7002/1

This organization is devoted to strengthening nonprofit boards. Its publications include *Fund Raising and the Nonprofit Board Member* and *A Snapshot of America's Nonprofit Boards.*

National Committee for Responsive Philanthropy
2001 S Street, NW, Suite 620
Washington, DC 20009
202-387-9177
http://www.primenet.com/~ncrp/index/html

This organization of local and national nonprofits seeks to improve the accountability and accessibility of philanthropic organizations and to increase the responsiveness of philanthropic organizations (that is, foundations) to organizations that are seeking to achieve social justice and fairer representation of those who are economically and politically disenfranchised. Its publications include *Responsive Philanthropy* and a variety of bulletins, action alerts, and occasional publications on charitable giving trends.

National Committee on Planned Giving
310 North Alabama Street, Suite 210
Indianapolis, IN 46202-2103
317-269-6274

This organization is concerned with planned giving. It publishes a range of resource materials on planned giving and a bimonthly newsletter entitled *Gift Planning Update*.

National Federation of Nonprofits
815 15th Street, NW, Suite 822
Washington, DC 20005-2201
202-628-4380

This organization provides technical assistance to and advocates on behalf of the nonprofit sector and publishes useful resource materials.

National Society of Fund-Raising Executives (NSFRE)
1101 King Street, Suite 700
Alexandria, VA 22314
1-800-666-3863
http://www.nsfre.org

This is the professional organization of fundraising executives, established to assist its members through promulgation of ethical standards for the management and direction of nonprofits' fundraising programs, providing a forum for consideration of issues of concern to professional fundraisers, and publication of information relevant to the profession. Its publications include the *NSFRE Journal* and *NSFRE News*.

The Society for Nonprofit Organizations
6314 Odana Road, Suite 1
Madison, WI 53719
608-274-9777
http://www.uwex.edu/danenet/snpo

This is a membership organization that provides information and resources to the nonprofit sector, encourages communication and sharing among nonprofit organizations, and fosters a sense of community in the sector. Publications include *Nonprofit World*, which is published bimonthly, and *Nonprofit World Funding Alert*, which is published monthly.

Periodical Publications

The Chronicle of Philanthropy
Published biweekly by The Chronicle of Philanthropy, 1255 23rd Street, NW, Washington, DC 20037; 1-800-842-7817

Contributions: The "How-to" Source for Nonprofit Professionals
Published bimonthly by Cambridge Fund Raising Associates, P.O. Box 336, Medfield, MA 02052-0336; 508-359-0019

Foundation & Corporate Funding Advantage
Published monthly by Progressive Business Publications, 370 Technology Drive, Malvern, PA 19355; 1-800-220-5000

Foundation News & Commentary
Published bimonthly by the Council on Foundations, Inc., 1828 L Street, NW, Washington, DC 20036; 202-466-6512

Grassroots Fundraising Journal
Published bimonthly; P.O. Box 11607, Berkeley, CA 94712; 510-704-8714

Nonprofit Management and Leadership
Published quarterly by Jossey-Bass Publishers, 350 Sansome Street, San Francisco, CA 94104-1342; 1-800-956-7739

Nonprofit and Voluntary Sector Quarterly
Published quarterly by Jossey-Bass Publishers, 350 Sansome Street, San Francisco, CA 94104-1342; 1-800-956-7739

Nonprofit Research News
Published quarterly by The Aspen Institute, 1333 New Hampshire Avenue, NW, Suite 1070, Washington, DC 20036; 202-736-5800

Nonprofit World
Published bimonthly by The Society for Nonprofit Organizations, 6314 Odana Road, Suite 1, Madison, WI 53719; 608-274-9777

Philanthropic Digest
Published by the American Prospect Research Association, 414 Plaza Drive, Suite 209, Westmont, IL 60559; 708-655-0177

What's Working in Nonprofit Fundraising
Published monthly by Progressive Business Publications, 370 Technology Drive, Malvern, PA 19355; 1-800-220-5000

Selected Books

Bame, K. (Ed.). (1996). *Corporate giving directory* (17th ed.). Rockville, MD: Taft Group.

Includes profiles on the largest corporate giving programs in the United States, as well as information about companies, their grant application processes, recent grants made, and how to contact them.

Barron, T. (Ed.). (1994). *Who's wealthy in America*. Rockville, MD: Taft Group.

Personal and financial information on America's wealthiest people (those with net worth of at least $1 million). Volume 1 includes personal information, and volume 2 includes information about stock holdings.

Baumgartner, J. E. (Ed.). (1995). *National directory of grantmaking public charities*. New York: The Foundation Center.

A guide to American foundations that make grants.

Carlson, M. (1995). *Winning grants step by step*. San Francisco: Jossey-Bass.

Support Centers of America's complete workbook for planning, developing, and writing successful proposals.

Conrad, D. L. (1995). *Corporate 500: Directory of corporate philanthropy* (13th ed.). San Francisco: Datarex Corporation.

Contribution profiles of corporations with major giving programs. Includes a business profile, information about application procedures, and sample grants; includes "Grants-at-a-Glance," section that provides a graphic summary of corporate giving programs.

Dove, K. E. (1988). *Conducting a successful capital campaign.* San Francisco: Jossey-Bass.

A comprehensive fundraising guide for nonprofit organizations.

Dun & Bradstreet. (1995). *Reference book of corporate managements.* Chicago: Author.

Profiles of corporate executives of those firms with the highest revenues in the United States. Includes biographical data and work history. Indexed geographically by Standard Industrial Classification code (SIC), by names, by college or university, and by military affiliation.

Duronio, M. A., & Tempel, E. R. (1996). *Fundraisers: Their careers, stories, concerns, and accomplishments.* San Francisco: Jossey-Bass.

Edles, L. P. (1993). *Fundraising: Hands-on tactics for nonprofit groups.* New York: McGraw-Hill.

General overview of fundraising strategies and techniques, including content on "getting your message across."

Ehr, C. M. (Ed.). (1993). *Owners and officers of private companies.* Rockville, MD: Taft Group.

Short business profiles on executives of private companies. Includes name, title, company name and address, and sales information. Indexed by company names, geographic areas, and Standard Industrial Classification code (SIC).

Ehr, C. M. (Ed.). (1994). *New fortunes.* Rockville, MD: Taft Group.

Contains biographical profiles of America's emerging wealth holders, including information about company sales, compensation figures, and insider stock holdings. Also includes information about individuals' rise to affluence and their charitable activities.

Fisher, H. S. (Ed.). (1995). *American salaries and wages survey.* Detroit, MI: Gale Research.

Lists salary and wage statistics for different jobs and occupations.

The Foundation Center. (1996/1997). *The foundation 1000.* New York: Author.

Comprehensive profiles on 1,000 of the most influential foundations in the United States plus updates on foundations profiled in the previous year.

Glynn, J. (Ed.). (1995). *Who knows who: Networking through corporate boards.* Detroit, MI: Gale Group.

Establishes the interconnections of corporate boards by listing board members' connections and company connections. Provides short profiles of each company including a list of the board of directors.

Graham, C. (1992). *Keep the money coming: A step by step strategic guide to annual fundraising.* Sarasota, FL: Pineapple Press.

A practical guide to annual fund strategies and techniques.

Greenfield, J. M. (1994). *Fund-raising fundamentals: A guide to annual giving for professionals and volunteers.* New York: John Wiley & Sons.

A comprehensive "how-to" book on annual giving.

Hall, L. V. (Ed.). (1995). *National directory of corporate giving* (4th ed.). New York: The Foundation Center.

Profiles of corporate foundations and giving programs. Indexed by personnel, business type, funding areas, geographic area, and company and program names.

Hammock, D. C., & Young, D. R. (Eds.). (1993). *Nonprofit organizations in a market economy: Understanding new roles, issues, trends.* San Francisco: Jossey-Bass.

An examination of the ways nonprofits act in the marketplace, including how nonprofits obtain necessary capital.

Hick, S. D. (Ed.). (1992). *Funding decisionmakers.* Rockville, MD: Taft Group.

Lists directors of foundations and civic organizations in the United States.

Horton, C. (1991). *Raising money & having fun (sort of): A "how to" book for small non-profit groups.* Cleveland, OH: The May Dugan Center.

Comprehensive, practical strategies, and techniques that can work for small nonprofits.

Howe, F. (1991). *The board member's guide to fund raising.* San Francisco: Jossey-Bass.

What every trustee needs to know about raising money.

Jankowski, K. E. (Ed.). (1992). *Directory of international corporate giving in America and abroad.* Rockville, MD: Taft Group.

Profiles of about 600 companies that are foreign-owned with operations in the United States and U.S.-owned with operations abroad.

Jankowski, K. E. (Ed.). (1992). *Inside Japanese support.* New York: Taft Group.

Profiles of Japanese corporate giving and foundation giving programs.

Jankowski, K. E. (Ed.). (1994). *America's new foundations.* Rockville, MD: Taft Group.

Profiles of more than 3,300 private, corporate, and community foundations created since 1980. Includes contact information, giving priorities, financial information, and major grants.

King, D. (1995). *Get the facts on anyone* (2nd ed.). New York: Macmillan.
Advice on how to research individuals.

Lawson, D. M. (1991). *Give to live: How giving can change your life*. LaJolla,
CA: ALTI Publishing.
A good book for volunteers and prospective donors that suggests
that if they give some of their time and money to desirable causes, they
will in return receive many personal rewards.

Maggard, M. (Ed.). (1993). *Guide to private fortunes*. Rockville, MD:
Taft Group.
Information on the wealthiest or most philanthropic people in the
United States who have a net worth of at least $25 million or have
demonstrated a history of generous charitable giving.

Oleck, H. L. (1988). *Nonprofit corporations, organizations, & associations*
(5th ed.). Englewood Cliffs, NJ: Prentice Hall.

Oleck, H. L., & Stewart, M. E. (1993). *1993 cumulative supplement*.
Englewood Cliffs, NJ: Prentice Hall.

Oleck, H. L., & Stewart, M. E. (1995). *1995/96 cumulative supplement*.
Englewood Cliffs, NJ: Prentice Hall.
These books provide an excellent overview of legal issues related
to nonprofits.

Patterson, K. (Ed.). (1994). *Who owns whom, North America* (Vol. 2).
Chicago: Dun & Bradstreet.
Information on parent companies and subsidiaries operating in the
United States and Canada.

Phelps, S. (Ed.). (1994). *Who's who among black Americans* (8th ed.).
Detroit, MI: Gale Research.
Biographical profiles of black Americans with exceptional achieve-
ments and contributions to society.

Prince, R. A., & File, K. M. (1994). *The seven faces of philanthropy: A new approach to cultivating major donors.* San Francisco: Jossey-Bass.

Categorizes wealthy donors into seven motivational types to help fundraisers better understand and cultivate major gift prospects.

Romaniuk, B. R. (Ed.). (1996). *1997 Foundation reporter.* Rockville, MD: Taft Group.

Detailed information on the leading private philanthropies in the United States (those having assets of at least $10 million). Includes contact information, financial profiles, contribution summaries, donor information, and application and review procedures.

Rosso, H. A. (1996). *Rosso on fund raising: Lessons from a master's lifetime experience.* San Francisco: Jossey-Bass.

Rosso, H. A., & Associates. (1991). *Achieving excellence in fund raising.* San Francisco: Jossey-Bass.

A comprehensive guide to principles, strategies, and methods.

Shaw, S. C., & Taylor, M. A. (1995). *Reinventing fundraising: Realizing the potential of women's philanthropy.* San Francisco: Jossey-Bass.

Strategies for involving women in philanthropic giving.

Shih, K. (Ed.). (1996). *Corporate yellow book.* New York: Leadership Directories.

Profiles of the top public corporations in the United States. Includes corporate headquarters information, top executives, subsidiaries, and board members. Indexed by state, industry type, company or subsidiary, and individual names.

Standard & Poor. (1995). *Standard & Poor's registry.* New York: Author.

Volume 1 profiles more than 55,000 corporations in and out of the United States. Volume 2 lists individual executives with personal and business information. Volume 3 indexes by geographic area, corporate family, and the Standard Industry Classification code (SIC).

Stetter, S. L. (Ed.). (1993). *Almanac of famous people* (5th ed.). Detroit, MI: Information Reference Group/Gale Research.

A two-volume guide to famous people in history; includes short biographies and chronological, geographic, and occupational indexes.

Unterburger, A. L. (Ed.). (1994). *Who's who among Asian Americans.* Detroit, MI: Gale Research.

Biographical profiles of Asian Americans with exceptional achievements and contributions to society.

Unterburger, A. L. (Ed.). (1994). *Who's who among Hispanic Americans* (3rd ed.). Detroit, MI: Gale Research.

Biographical profiles of Hispanic Americans with exceptional achievements and contributions to society.

Walsh, E. T. (Ed.). (1996). *Corporate directory of U.S. public companies.* San Mateo, CA: Walkers Western Research.

Information on public corporations, indexed by officer or director, owner, state, Standard Industry Classification code (SIC) number, stock exchange symbol, and newly registered corporations. Includes salary information.

Warwick, M. (1994). *How to write successful fundraising letters.* Berkeley, CA: Strathmoor Press.

Practical suggestions for writing effective fundraising letters.

THE FOUNDATION CENTER LIBRARY SERVICES

The Foundation Center disseminates current information on foundation and corporate giving through its national collections in New York and Washington, DC, as well as through its field offices in Atlanta, Cleveland, and San Francisco and its network of approximately 200 cooperating libraries in all 50 states and abroad. These library collections provide grant seekers with free access to core Foundation Center publications as well as a wide range of books, periodicals, and research documents relating to philanthropy.

National Collections

79 Fifth Avenue
New York, NY 10003-3076
212-620-4230
http://fdncenter.org

1001 Connecticut Avenue, NW
Suite 938
Washington, DC 20036
202-331-1400

Field Offices

Suite 150, Hurt Building
50 Hurt Plaza
Atlanta, GA 30303-2914
404-880-0094

312 Sutter Street
San Francisco, CA 94108
415-397-0902

1536 Hanna Building
1422 Euclid Avenue
Cleveland, OH 44115
216-861-1934

THE COMPLEAT PROFESSIONAL'S LIBRARY

The following helpful publications are available for purchase from The Compleat Professional's Library:

Big Gifts
Black Tie Optional
Complete Book of Model Fund Raising Letters
Designs for Fund Raising
Federal Money Retriever (software)
Games for Fund Raising
Going . . . Going . . . Gone!
Golf Tournament Management Manual
Hands-on Guide to FR Strategy & Evaluation
How to Write Successful Fund Raising Letters
Pinpointing Affluence
Planned Giving: Management, Marketing, & Law
Raising Money by Mail
Take the Fear Out of Asking for Major Gifts
Where the Money Is

For a price list, complete catalog, or ordering information, contact The Compleat Professional's Library, P.O. Box 336, Medfield, MA 02052-0336. Telephone: 508-359-0019.

INDEX

ABOUT THE AUTHORS

Richard L. Edwards, PhD, ACSW, is dean and professor, School of Social Work, University of North Carolina at Chapel Hill. A former president of NASW, he serves on nonprofit boards of trustees and frequently provides training and consultation on nonprofit management and fundraising issues.

Elizabeth A. S. Benefield, BA, is assistant dean for development and external affairs, School of Social Work, University of North Carolina at Chapel Hill. She serves on nonprofit boards of trustees, teaches fundraising courses and workshops, and consults on fundraising issues.

Jeffrey A. Edwards, BA, is prospect research analyst, Office of Development, University of North Carolina at Chapel Hill. He provides consultation on prospect issues for nonprofits.

John A. Yankey, PhD, is Leonard W. Mayo Professor, Mandel School of Applied Social Sciences, and faculty director of the Governance and Management Consulting Clinic at the Mandel Center for Nonprofit Organizations, Case Western Reserve University, Cleveland, Ohio. He has served on the boards of trustees of many nonprofit organizations and frequently consults on nonprofit management and fundraising issues.

Building a Strong Foundation: Fundraising for Nonprofits

Cover designed by The Watermark Design Office
Interior designed by Naylor Design, Inc.
Composed by Wolf Publications, Inc., in Jenson and Myriad
Printed by Graphic Communications, Inc., on 60# Finch Offset

BOOKS ON MANAGEMENT BY THE NASW PRESS

Building a Strong Foundation: Fundraising for Nonprofits, *by Richard L. Edwards and Elizabeth A. S. Benefield, with Jeffrey A. Edwards and John A. Yankey*

Addresses all the aspects necessary to raise funds successfully in a nonprofit environment. Learn how to build the relationships that are central to successful fundraising activities.

ISBN: 0-87101-249-9. Item #2499. Price $27.95

New Management in Human Services, Second Edition, *Leon Ginsberg and Paul R. Keys, Editors*

Offers guidance on how to work with boards, boost staff morale, work with the media, improve service delivery, and more. It also gives advice to help managers stay focused, maintain a high energy level, and control stress.

ISBN: 0-87101-251-0. Item #2510. Price $31.95

Interactional Supervision, *by Lawrence Shulman*

Presents practical strategies for formal and informal supervision.

ISBN: 0-87101-220-0. Item #2200. Price $34.95

Skills for Effective Human Services Management, *Richard L. Edwards and John A. Yankey, Editors*

Provides skills-building techniques and practice exercises to increase and sharpen management skills.

ISBN: 0-87101-195-6. Item #1956. Price $34.95

Changing Hats: From Social Work Practice to Administration, *by Felice Davidson Perlmutter*

Examines the challenges faced by direct practitioners who move from practice into management.

ISBN: 0-87101-184-0. Item #1840. $23.95

(Order form on reverse side)

ORDER FORM

Title	Item #	Price	Total
__ Building a Strong Foundation	Item 2499	$27.95	_____
__ New Management in Human Services	Item 2510	$31.95	_____
__ Interactional Supervision	Item 2200	$34.95	_____
__ Skills for Effective Human Services Management	Item 1956	$34.95	_____
__ Changing Hats	Item 1840	$23.95	_____
		Subtotal	_____
	+ 10% postage and handling		_____
		Total	_____

❏ I've enclosed my check or money order for $ _____.

❏ Please charge my ❏ NASW Visa* ❏ Other Visa ❏ MasterCard

_____   _____

Credit Card Number   Expiration Date

Signature _____

Use of this card generates funds in support of the social work profession.

Name_____

Address _____

City _____ State/Province _____

Country _____ Zip _____

Phone _____   _____

NASW Member # (if applicable)

(Please make checks payable to NASW Press. Prices are subject to change.)

NASW PRESS

NASW Press
P.O. Box 431
Annapolis JCT, MD 20701
USA

Credit card orders call
1-800-227-3590
(In the Metro Wash., DC, area, call 301-317-8688)
Or fax your order to 301-206-7989
Or e-mail nasw@pmds.com

Visit our Web site at http://www.naswpress.org   BSFBI96